— Praise for *The Century-Old Startup* —

The Century-Old Startup offers an insightful exploration into what it takes to adapt and sustain business success. Best-selling author and Nordstrom expert Robert Spector artfully demonstrates how Nordstrom has thrived for a century thanks to adherence to unwavering core values and a passion for relentless evolution. Moreover, Robert provides a blueprint for your company's sustainability and growth. *The Century-Old Startup* is a must-read book for leaders and entrepreneurs who want to position their companies for credibility, relevance, uniqueness, and durability.

—Joseph Michelli, Ph.D., *New York Times* #1 bestselling author of *The New Gold Standard* and *The Airbnb Way*

Robert Spector has taken everything he's learned over the past 30-plus years studying one of the great companies of our time and distilled it into an insightful set of principles that anyone can understand. If you want to build a culture of hospitality that will stand the test of time, you need to read this book.

—Will Guidara, Restaurateur and author of *Unreasonable Hospitality*

This literary gem teaches us invaluable skills to navigate the choppy waters of an uncertain economy. Its pages brim with practical wisdom, and transcend the confines of any industry, offering FACTS as a blueprint for thriving in any economy.

—Simon T. Bailey, Author of *Ignite the Power of Women in Your Life*

Robert Spector, the expert on all things Nordstrom, is back with more lessons we can learn from one of the most iconic brands on the planet, known for its legendary customer service. Read this book before your competition does!

—Shep Hyken, Customer service/CX expert and *New York Times* bestselling author

Robert Spector has bottled up and packaged up for us the illusive formula for sustainable legacy, customer love and admiration, and growth. By opening up the actions behind the outcomes that the beloved Nordstrom brand through world wars, the Great Depression, recessions, changing consumer desires, succession and even AI; he provides a playbook to emulate and lead by their example.

—JEANNE BLISS, Author of *Chief Customer Officer 2.0* and *Would You Do That to Your Mother?*

Great role models not only give us prototypes to emulate, but they also inform us of what is possible. Nordstrom has been a noble exemplar of great customer experience for over a hundred years— one that has changed with the times yet remain grounded in its original core values. Robert Spector, the foremost expert on all things Nordstrom, has given us a powerful yet practical roadmap for every organization to become more like Nordstrom.

—CHIP R. BELL, Author of *Inside Your Customer's Imagination*

Robert Spector continues to update the story of this brilliant family-run business with his inimitable combination of warmth, humility and storytelling whilst delivering frank commentary and deep insight. Importantly, the writing is backed up with a unique access to the family's perspective spanning four generations. Nordstrom has become synonymous with service excellence across industry sectors. In *The Century-Old Startup* Robert explains the power of organizations first having crystal clarity about who they are and what they stand for, and then setting about making this a practical reality, focusing on doing it rather than talking about it. And anyone who can sum up the whole message of the book with a brilliant Bob Dylan quote gets my vote!

—ALAN WILLIAMS, Author of *Supercharging The Customer Experience*

Robert Spector has done it again! He's created a book that revels in the joy and significance of delivering a superior customer service experience while providing a primer and guidebook for entrepreneurs embarking on the launch a new product or brand. This book illuminates the mindset needed to build a brand that is not only viable in today's market, but that has the staying power—utilizing flexibility, agility, communication, transformation and social responsibility—to thrive and succeed for decades to come.

This ain't your average customer service book. Robert Spector has mined the brilliance of the Nordstrom mindset and presents readers with a roadmap for anyone building a new company or embarking on a new launch. Not only does he highlight the beauty and significance of fully committing to the customer service experience, he also shines a light on what a business must do to survive, thrive, and eventually become a household name decades after launch. If you are an entrepreneur, you need to know these insights; they are invaluable.

—KATE EDWARDS, Executive coach, speaker, and author of
Hello! And Every Little Thing That Matters

Retail historically is about birth, life, death, and compost. Look at the top ten list of retail empires of the past forty years and note the death rate. Bed Bath and Beyond lasted how many years? Remember Sears and Kmart? Retail is about change. What made a good store even ten years ago and what makes a good one today are so different. The impact of gender roles, the ubiquity of screens, much less the role of fashion. Nordstrom has lasted a long time and prospered by staying ahead of the curve. Robert Spector has documented that effort. This book is a good read for all of us in a rapidly changing world.

—PACO UNDERHILL, Author of *Why We Buy* and *How We Eat*

— ALSO BY ROBERT SPECTOR —

THE NORDSTROM WAY: *The Inside Story of America's Number One Customer Service Company*

THE NORDSTROM WAY TO CUSTOMER SERVICE EXCELLENCE: *A Handbook for Implementing Great Service in Your Organization*

THE NORDSTROM WAY TO CUSTOMER SERVICE EXCELLENCE: *The Handbook for Becoming the "Nordstrom" of Your Industry*

THE NORDSTROM WAY TO CUSTOMER EXPERIENCE EXCELLENCE: *Creating a Values-Driven Service Culture*

AMAZON.COM: *Get Big Fast: Inside the Revolutionary Business Model That Changed the World*

CATEGORY KILLERS: *The Retail Revolution and Its Impact on Consumer Culture*

ANYTIME, ANYWHERE: *How the Best Bricks-and Clicks Businesses Deliver Seamless Service to Their Customers*

THE PIZZA HUT STORY

THE LEGEND OF EDDIE BAUER

THE MOM & POP STORE: *True Stories From the Heart of America*

THE
CENTURY-OLD STARTUP

THE NORDSTROM WAY
OF EMBRACING CHANGE, CHALLENGES,
AND A CULTURE OF CUSTOMER SERVICE

ROBERT SPECTOR
FOREWORD BY STEVE MADDEN

GAMZU

INCORPORATED

Bellingham, WA

10 9 8 7 6 5 4 3 2 1

Library of Congress Control Number: 2023916003

ISBN: 979-8-9890213-0-7 (Paperback)
ISBN: 979-8-9890213-1-4 (eBook)

Cover Photos: John W. Nordstrom,
used with permission of Nordstrom, Inc.
Nordstrom Local: Mehran Torgoley

Illustrations: Keith Bendis
Cover design: Scott Book
Book design: Melissa Vail Coffman

For my friend Bruce Nordstrom, a great man and a good man,
who taught me so much about The Nordstrom Way.

May your hands always be busy
May your feet always be swift
May you have a strong foundation
When the winds of changes shift

— **Bob Dylan,** *Forever Young*

Contents

Author's Notes ix

Nordstrom Family Chronology xi

Foreword xiii

Introduction xvii

    FLEXIBILITY 1

    AGILITY 35

    COMMUNICATION 71

    TRANSFORMATION 95

    SOCIAL RESPONSIBILITY 127

Acknowledgments 147

About the Author 149

Eyes may be the windows to the soul,
But shoes are the gateway to the psyche.

— **Linda O'Keefe**, *Shoes: A Celebration of Pumps,
Sandals, Slippers & More*

Author's Notes

The two photos on the cover of this book illustrate Nordstrom's century-plus journey—from a simple single shoe store in downtown Seattle to an omnichannel national chain that includes one of the finest stores in Manhattan. The top photo, used with the permission of Nordstrom, shows founder John W. Nordstrom in front of the Wallin & Nordstrom store in the 1920s. The bottom photo, taken a century later in Newport Beach, California, by photographer Mehran Torgoley, is of the company's unique customer service store, Nordstrom Local, which will be covered in detail in this narrative.

The majority of the content in this narrative comes from exclusive original interviews conducted by the author over the course of several years, including conversations with Pete, Erik and Jamie Nordstrom specifically for this book. Some quotes from the late Jim Nordstrom are taken from his 1996 interviews with the author. Portions of some of the other quotes originally appeared in *The Immigrant in 1887* by founder John W. Nordstrom; *A Winning Team* by John W.'s son Elmer, which covers the life and careers of the second generation of brothers Everett, Elmer and Lloyd; *Leave It Better Than You Found It* by Bruce Nordstrom (son of Everett) which covers the contributions of the third generation of Bruce, John N., Jim and Jack McMillan; *Mr. John* by Elmer's son John N., which chronicled his life inside and outside of the company; and the author's four books that comprise *The Nordstrom Way* series.

Nordstrom Family Chronology

AS YOU WILL LEARN FROM THIS narrative, over the course of four generations there were (and are) many Nordstroms. Throughout this book each will be referred to by only their first names. If you are uninterested in keeping track, just think of them as one generic Nordstrom. Believe or not, they are all humble enough to prefer that designation.

For the record, this is how they line up:

First generation: John W. (1871 — 1963)

Second generation: Everett (1903 — 1972)

                                Elmer (1904 — 1992)

                                Lloyd (1910 — 1974)

Third generation: Bruce (Everett's son; 1933 —)

                                John N. (Elmer's son; 1937 —)

                                James ("Jim"; Elmer's son, 1940 — 1996)

                                John "Jack" McMillan (Lloyd's son-in-law; 1935 — 2022)

Fourth generation: Blake (Bruce's son; 1960 — 2019)

                                Pete (Bruce's son; 1962 —)

                                Erik (Bruce's son; 1963 —)

                                Jamie (Jim's son; 1972 —)

Foreword

IREMEMBER WALKING INTO A NORDSTROM STORE as a young shoe designer. At that point, I barely had a company. The entire Steve Madden brand was really just a few shoes that I sold out of the trunk of a 1985 Nissan Sentra. But those shoes were stylish, affordable, and unique, and I'm thankful that was enough to convince the buyers at Nordstrom to take a chance on me.

Back then, Nordstrom had a different buyer in the shoe department at every single store. I can't stress enough how uncommon this was. It was unlike any other retailer, particularly in the shoe departments. Those buyers ran their floors and knew what their local customers wanted better than anyone. It was amazing.

To sell my shoes, I went to the different Nordstrom locations to call on the individual buyers. This allowed me to see what these stores all had in common, and the number one thing that they shared was their exceptional commitment to customer service. These were the smoking days, and I can still picture the big ashtrays they had strategically placed around the floor. Meanwhile, the sales associates took great care of each and every customer. Everything was set up down to the finest detail to maximize the customers' satisfaction.

Many of those employees that started off on the floor ended up working their way up the ranks. They and the people around them saw that hard work paid off. This engendered a deep sense of loyalty and pride in the brand that I witnessed several times. Several years ago, I mentioned wanting to buy a piece of jewelry, and the head shoe buyer not only walked me to the jewelry department, but he stayed with me the whole time to make sure that I was well taken care of and that I got exactly what I wanted. It truly felt like my experience was important to him. He wasn't getting a commission; this wasn't his department. He just really cared.

Another time, in the 1990s, I was speaking to a Divisional Merchandise Manager on the East Coast, who was describing the new flagship store that was being built in Seattle, the birthplace of Nordstrom. As he went into great detail about the design and plans for the store, he grew teary-eyed. I remember thinking to myself in that moment, "If only I could have employees like that. This is exactly how I want my company to be."

Over the years, I took a note from Nordstrom and nurtured our employees' growth at Steve Madden, hoping to gain that same sort of loyalty and pride. Amelia Newton Varela, who is now the President of our company, started in customer service, and our Chief Merchandising Officer Karla Frieders came from the front lines, selling to customers on the floor. I like to think that they—and other employees—feel similarly about Steve Madden to the way the Nordstrom team feels about their brand.

I also like to think that I've learned a few things about how to be a great leader from the former and, sadly, deceased President of the company, Blake Nordstrom. When I met Blake, he was the shoe buyer for the Seattle store. As I showed him my shoes, he sat across from me, propping his briefcase up on his lap to use it as a desk. I thought to myself, "He's a Nordstrom!"

He was an executive, but he was right there in the trenches buying directly from me, and he was incredibly humble. This translated into how he ran every aspect of the company. He was the kind of leader that answered every email and every phone call, and he personified the Nordstrom spirit.

More than anything, I learned from Blake—and from Nordstrom as a whole—that the details are just as important as the big picture. A great leader has to focus equally on both. His younger brothers, Pete and Erik, continue to follow Blake's example, which is the essence of *The Nordstrom Way*.

In *The Century-Old Startup*, Robert Spector gives countless examples of how four generations of Nordstroms have focused on the details—big and small. That focus has enabled this unique company to deal head-on with the inevitable ups and downs of life, both business and personal.

There's a line from the W. H. Auden poem, "As I Walked Out One Evening," that encapsulates how I feel about business: "A crack in the rim of a teacup leads to the land of the dead." A company's success lives and dies in the details. All of the Nordstrom leaders have understood this implicitly, and I carry its lesson with me every day at Steve Madden.

STEVE MADDEN
Creative and Design Chief,
Steve Madden, Ltd.
New York City

Introduction

*T*O MAKE CUSTOMERS FEEL GOOD *and look their best.* These nine simple words capture Nordstrom's official core mission.

Beginning with its modest founding as a shoe store in 1901, America's leading fashion department store has always adhered to the words of Aristide Boucicault, the itinerant 19th century peddler who in 1872 Paris created the Bon Marche, the world's first department store: "The client is the most important person in the store. She does not depend on us; we depend on her."

In other words, running a successful business is all about valuing the customer.

People often ask me: "What is the essence of *The Nordstrom Way?*"

It's simple. While most companies are predominantly transactional in nature, Nordstrom's overarching purpose is to establish a personal and lasting relationship with customers built on value, respect, trust and loyalty. How best to serve customers is at the core of every initiative and every strategic decision. Wherever customer interaction happens—be it in brick-and-mortar stores or on digital devices—the personal touch of customer service is central to the bond with that customer.

People nod in understanding, then follow up with, "And what else?"

To which I reply, "That's it."

THE NORDSTROM WAY

MY FIRST PROFESSIONAL CONTACT WITH NORDSTROM was in 1982 when I was a regular contributor to the trade newspapers *Women's Wear Daily* and *Footwear News*. At that time, Nordstrom was a strictly West Coast chain. Nevertheless, it was attracting national attention from Harvard Business School, which published a 1979 case study on the company, with a heavy focus on the culture. Tom Peters, co-author of the seminal 1982 book *In Search of Excellence: Lessons from America's Best-Run Companies*, frequently wrote and spoke about Nordstrom's customer service.

Around that same time, *Forbes* magazine, referencing the nickname of New York's Bloomingdale's department store, dubbed the retailer from the Pacific Northwest "Bloomies in the Boonies."

> Nordstrom has become a metaphor. Companies boast they are "The Nordstrom" of their industry.

As a native of New Jersey (where customer service remains a novel concept), whose first job out of college was writing retail advertising for the Newark-based Bamberger's department store chain (then a division of Macy's), I was fascinated by the Nordstrom culture of motivated, entrepreneurial, commission-driven salespeople dedicated to going above and beyond expectations to satisfy customers and build loyal relationships.

Nordstrom has become a metaphor. Many companies across the United States boast that they are "The Nordstrom" of their particular industry. Some examples I've found over the years: "The Nordstrom of Real Estate," "The Nordstrom of Funeral Homes" (satisfaction guaranteed?) and my very favorite, "The Nordstrom of Garbage."

In 1995, with the cooperation of Nordstrom (both the family and the company), I wrote *The Nordstrom Way: The Inside Story of America's Number One Customer Service Company*, assisted by Patrick D. McCarthy, then Nordstrom's top salesperson. The book became a bestseller and led me to write a series of completely different books:

- *The Nordstrom Way to Customer Service Excellence: A Handbook for Implementing Great Service in Your Organization* (2005)

- *The Nordstrom Way to Customer Service Excellence: The Handbook for Becoming the "Nordstrom" of Your Industry* (Second Edition, 2012)

- *The Nordstrom Way to Customer Experience Excellence: Creating a Values-Driven Service Culture* (Third Edition, 2017)

They are linked by the common theme of exploring Nordstrom's culture, which is built upon an unwavering commitment to creating a memorable experience for both employees and customers. Nordstrom continues to be relevant by anticipating, studying, and adjusting to changes in the marketplace, particularly customer service which, "is not defined by us based on our legacy practices," said Pete Nordstrom, President and Chief Brand Officer. "It's defined by customers."

As of this writing, Nordstrom has 94 full-line stores (down from a pre-pandemic total of 116), 245 Nordstrom Rack off-price stores across the country, as well as seven Nordstrom Local service stores in Los Angeles (five) and Manhattan (two), and a strong online presence that generates more than 40 percent of annual company sales of more than $15 billion.

Dollar-for-dollar, Nordstrom is one of the greatest stories in the history of American business. Publicly traded for more than half a century, family-run by four generations since 1901, we will never see its like again.

The old adage about family businesses goes like this:

- First generation builds it

- Second generation enjoys it

- Third generation destroys it

Never mentioned is the fourth generation because companies rarely last that long. That's one reason why Nordstrom is exceptional.

Enduring companies deal head-on with whatever challenges come their way. As you will read in this narrative, there have been many turning points in Nordstrom's 120-plus years: World War I, the Great Depression, World War II, various recessions, a well-publicized 1990 labor dispute, succession issues, premature deaths of family leaders, the ever-changing world of fashion, the rise and impact of its Seattle neighbor Amazon, the aftermath of the George Floyd murder in Minneapolis, and the COVID-19 pandemic that began in early 2020.

What makes Nordstrom's story so powerful and remarkable is that each generation has been the perfect fit for its time. Each generation has had the experience, commitment, motivation and knowledge to make their mark—to survive and stay relevant —and to build on the twin legacies of family and company. If that was not the response to all their challenges, Nordstrom would have been consigned to the crowded graveyard of once proud retailers such as Marshall Field, Dayton's, Gimbel's, Hudson's, The Broadway, Abraham & Straus, B. Altman, Bullock's, Kaufmann's, Rich's, and countless others.

One long-ago, now-forgotten, retail powerhouse named Carter Hawley Hale Stores came within a hair of buying Nordstrom from brothers Everett, Elmer and Lloyd in 1970. That potential transaction will be discussed in greater detail. If that sale had happened, you would not be reading this book.

As of this writing, the odds are stacked against Nordstrom being led by a fifth-generation family member. Most of that generation are either too young or have sought their own path outside the company. With eyes trained on the next phase of its journey, and not on the finish line, current management has long been addressing the challenge of non-family leadership.

"Erik and I could run out the clock for our generation, but we're playing the long game," Pete told me. "It's always been in our mind that it's not about us; it's not a finite time frame. We have a responsibility to make Nordstrom an evergreen proposition. We always look to the future to see how we can remain relevant."

THE CENTURY-OLD STARTUP

WHY IS THIS BOOK CALLED *The Century-Old Startup*? While Nordstrom is not technically a startup, its culture has always been driven by an entrepreneurial energy and a desire to disrupt its industry by offering customer service that can rarely be equal.

Following its core value of being "Curious and Ever Changing," Nordstrom, according to company literature, "approaches problems with curiosity and creates solutions. We unlock potential to be bold, think big and inspire innovation. We *disrupt the status quo* [emphasis mine] to solve customer needs in new and relevant ways." Those are the hallmarks of a startup.

Throughout its history, Nordstrom has always acted as if it was a new business, asking itself, "If we started our business today, what would it look like?"

Transformation is essential to survival. A fundamental theme of this book is that any company in any industry that aspires to endure must be in a perpetual state of transformation. If you're standing still, you're falling behind. Nordstrom is not the same company today that it was five years ago. It will be a different company five years from now.

What will your organization look like five years from now?

> Nordstrom adjusts practices according to times and markets; it holds fast to core values that support its culture.

CULTURE IS THE BALLAST

AFTER ALL IS SAID AND DONE, the Nordstrom story begins and ends with one word: *culture*.

Culture is the ballast—the substantial weight that steadies the metaphorical ship through the business world's raging storms and roiling seas. Competitiveness is essential to the culture. Throughout its history, Nordstrom has been unafraid to eschew once-successful practices that no longer were effective or relevant. While Nordstrom adjusts its practices according to changing times and mutable markets, it holds fast to core values that underpin its culture.

Values are standards of behavior, the nonnegotiable beliefs that are most important in your life.

If "vision" is the head, and "mission" is the heart, then "values" are the soul of your culture. The only way an organization can create a lasting customer service culture is by hiring people who buy into the core values.

Most organizations are guided by practices that are influenced by market conditions, such as short-term strategies for product and/or service offerings. In order to stay competitive, you must adjust your way of doing business. Your organization's viability is *designed* by your business plan, but your longevity is *determined* by your personal values, which represent what you are as an organization.

"Values define who we are, and if they change we become something else," said Pete, who described practices as, "ways of doing things . . . that express our values. Practices may serve us well for long periods of time—but they are *not* values and, therefore, can be changed without changing our culture. So, if we're thinking about the business from the customers' point of view, we should evolve and be nimble and provide the goods or services that they are looking for. There are very few things that are sacred; that we should stay true to. Practices, which change and evolve, deliver these values."

By adhering to a set of nonnegotiable values any organization can attract and retain the people who will help you achieve success. Once you identify the kind of people that will thrive in your organization, you will be happy only with those who share your values. I'm not talking about people who think as you do, but rather people who already believe as you do.

CHANGE

"EVERY SUCCESSFUL ORGANIZATION HAS TO MAKE the transition from a world defined primarily by repetition to one primarily defined by change," according to Bill Drayton, the American social entrepreneur. "This is the biggest transformation in the structure of how humans work together since the Agricultural Revolution."

Although much has changed in how Nordstrom conducts its business since its founding in 1901, what hasn't changed is the company's laser-like focus on customer service, and—more important—the evolution of what customer service means in our omnichannel world. Unchanged are the strength and power of a unique culture that is referenced, revered, and reinforced by leadership at every level, carried out by motivated salespeople, and solidified by satisfied customers.

"Our culture around service was established long before any of us were around," said Erik, the Chief Executive Officer, and a member of the fourth generation. "We are the fortunate recipients of it."

Although they didn't invent the way Nordstrom does business, Pete and Erik see their job as keeping the company modern, relevant, and interesting.

"The strength of our culture and the loyalty of our customers have always sustained us through tough times and enabled us to pivot to whatever the future holds," said Pete. "Because our cultural foundation is centered on what's relevant to customers, it's easy for us to pivot and to keep thinking long-term. *The customer is still the best filter we have for every business decision we make.*" [Emphasis mine]

For members of the Nordstrom family, "Our personal reputation is hard to distinguish from the reputation of the company," said Jamie, Chief Merchandising Officer. "Therefore, we are highly motivated to preserve and protect the reputation of the business, because that's also our reputation. If someone has a bad experience at Nordstrom it's personal. Not because we made it personal; it just is."

WHY THIS BOOK?

COVID-19 TRIGGERED MANY UNEXPECTED THINGS. This book is one of them. Observing how Erik and Pete led the company through the unprecedented, uncertain times of 2020 and beyond—a worldwide pandemic and a reckoning on race relations in America—I was impressed by the brothers' focus and transparency on maintaining company-wide morale and a positive view of the future. And this was at a time when they and their co-workers were still reeling from the sudden and unexpected death in 2019 of their older brother Blake, the co-president with Pete and Erik. (I will be going into greater detail about Blake and his extraordinary impact on the company, particularly employees on the frontlines.)

During the extended period that company stores were closed, and executives worked from home, it was essential for Erik and Pete to communicate with employees in the U.S. and Canada. Every Friday for months, the brothers conducted an online broadcast to all employees to keep them abreast of the current state of the company and to prepare them for the post-pandemic future—even though no one knew for certain what the future would look like.

Take risks and be open to change.

From the start, taking risks and being open to change have been essential to the Nordstrom way. Beginning with founder John W., every generation has been comfortable with using innovation and adaptation to help meet existential challenges. Despite the post-COVID challenges, Nordstrom still made *Fortune* magazine's list of "Most Admired Companies In The World" for the 14th year in a row, based on investment value, quality of management and products, commitments to social responsibility, and ability to attract talent. I'm not in the prediction business but based on the company's century-plus track record—and because of the principles described in this book—I expect Nordstrom to continue to survive and thrive, because, well, that's what Nordstrom does.

The impact of COVID. "taught us the value of knowing who we are and what we stand for," Erik told shareholders in May 2022. "In the face of continuing uncertainty, both within our industry and around the world, we kept our focus and priorities clear: *Nordstrom exists to help customers feel good and look their best.*"

Pete and Erik's leadership inspired me to look at how previous generations of Nordstroms handled adversity in their day. I thought, "this is a book."

After writing four different books and countless articles and speaking about the company to audiences in 30 countries all over the globe, you might think that I've penned and pontificated everything I have to say. But you would be wrong. There's plenty more to explore. Based on my 40-plus years of studying Nordstrom, I believe the company's success is built around the acronym F.A.C.T.S., which are the keys to an enduring culture of customer service and represent the chapters of this book:

- **Flexibility:** Always responding and adjusting to change

- **Agility:** Nimbleness and dexterity

- **Communication:** Clear, frequent messaging of information, purpose, goals, and praise

- **Transformation:** Continually evaluating product offerings, services and market strategies

- **Social Responsibility:** Being an aspirational company for those who want to work for—and do business with—corporate citizens that share their social values

These characteristics are not unrelated silos. Flexibility, Agility and Transformation can't exist without each other—and none could happen without Communication. Social Responsibility helps to bind the culture for employees, business partners and, most important, customers.

So now, here are the F.A.C.T.S.

FLEXIBILITY

the quality of bending easily without breaking

F

Flexibility is the key to stability.

— **John Wooden**, legendary UCLA basketball coach

"A T NORDSTROM, YOU LEARN TO LIVE in the gray area," a long-time company salesperson once told me. "Living with ambiguity is challenging, but in the end it keeps our responses to people and issues very real. Who knows what curveball gets thrown at us a week from now?"

Flexibility is essential to responding to uncertainty.

When the future is unfathomable, "tolerance of ambiguity" is one of the most important qualities found in top leaders according to the Korn Ferry Institute, which studies trends and drivers of human and organizational performance.

"Tolerance of ambiguity" extends to measuring risk-taking, innovation, openness to differences, financial strength and social responsibility. Resilient organizations respond to challenges even when the solutions might not yet be clear or articulated. Confidence and commitment in the face of uncertainty defines how Nordstrom has survived and thrived.

Pursing the American Dream

Flexibility begins with Johan Wilhelm Nordstrom, the middle child of five, born in 1871 in the town of Alvik Neder Lulea, in northernmost Sweden, sixty miles below the Arctic Circle.

Johan's father, who was a blacksmith, wagon maker, and part-time farmer, passed away in 1879 when Johan was eight years old. According to his father's will, Johan and his mother received half the farm. Johan's older brother received the other half, but his share consisted of the house, the barn and other farm buildings. Eventually Johan grew weary of his second-class status within his family. His tale became the quintessential immigrant story. He left Sweden for America in 1887 at the age of 16, with 450 crowns (about $112.00) in his pocket. After arriving at Ellis Island, where an immigration official purportedly anglicized his name to "John," he made his way across America, eventually reaching the budding town of Seattle in 1895. Along the way, he was flexible enough to find work wherever he could—laborer, logger, coal miner, silver miner, gold miner, and farmer.

Without realizing it, John W, had created the template for the Nordstrom ambition and work ethic that extends to today. No job is too small to be unimportant to success. Today, the highest recognition at Nordstrom is the John W. Nordstrom Award, which goes to the manager who most exemplifies the characteristics of the founder, which the company lists as "hard work, persistence, servant leadership, loyalty, honesty, ethics, competitive spirit, and an unwavering commitment to putting the customer first."

After a couple of years working a farm north of Seattle, John W. changed the course of his life when he decided to gamble on himself. In 1897, gold had been discovered in the Klondike region of Canada's Yukon Territory, more than one thousand miles away from Seattle. John W. collected his belongings and, "what little I had and by four o'clock that afternoon I was on the train bound for Seattle and a new adventure," he wrote in his memoir, *The Immigrant in 1887*. Billing itself as the "Gateway to the Yukon," Seattle was an embarkation point and source of supplies for tens of thousands of other men lured by the promise of riches up north. (The retailers who sold the supplies generally made out better than the prospectors themselves.)

A week after arriving in Seattle, John W. boarded the coal freighter *Willamette* for the journey north to Port Valdez, along with 1,200 men, 600 horses and 600 mules. Because he could afford only second-class passage, he slept with the horses and mules. His ultimate destination was Dawson, the swelling frontier town in the heart of the gold fields. On his trek, John W. battled bitter cold, snow, rain, storms and wind, mostly on foot because his horse had died along the way and had to be butchered for food.

Who knew this trek would eventually lead to a world of Chanel handbags, Alexander McQueen gowns and Christian Louboutin shoes?

For the next two years, John W. struggled in the gold fields, supporting himself with various odd jobs. (Flexibility) Finally, his luck changed when he hit a gold strike. But after John W. staked his claim, another miner challenged it. Claim disputes were settled by the Canadian Gold Commission. Unfortunately for John W., the Gold Commissioner was the brother of the other miner. (Corruption was not unknown in the Yukon.) John W.'s friends advised him to sell his claim to the other man, rather than hold out and possibly wind up with nothing. After paying his legal expenses, the 29-year-old Swede ended up with about $13,000 (more than $400,000 in today's dollars), which "looked like a lot of money to me," he wrote in his memoir, and returned to Seattle, which was a young, get-rich-quick boom town offering a host of commercial possibilities.

John W. invested in some Seattle real estate and went to business college. In May 1900, he married Hilda Carlson, a Swedish girl he had dated a few times before going to Alaska. John and Hilda (who had been working as a domestic) were part of the growing group of Scandinavian immigrants who were drawn to the Puget Sound's climate and scenery, and the fishing and logging that was similar to those of their homeland. Their pragmatism and work ethic contributed to the make-up of Seattle in general and Nordstrom in particular.

John W. often visited an old Klondike acquaintance named Carl F. Wallin, who ran a ten-foot-wide shoe repair shop on Second Avenue in downtown Seattle. Wallin suggested that he and Nordstrom form a partnership in a retail shoe store that would be established on the site of the repair shop. Nordstrom agreed, putting up $5,000; Wallin added $1,000. Some of the money was used to fix up the store, which was immediately expanded to twenty feet. With $3,500, they bought an inventory of shoes and, in 1901, opened Wallin & Nordstrom on Fourth Avenue and Pike Street. (I've always wondered why Wallin got top billing.)

"The store was so small and looked so poor that the fellows from the better factories back East wouldn't even call on us to sell us shoes," John W. wrote in his memoir.

Everett, Elmer and Lloyd lived and identified with the values and principles that eventually became *The Nordstrom Way.*

Nevertheless, Wallin & Nordstrom grew to a prosperous little business, comprising one shoe store downtown and a second store four miles away near the bustling University of Washington campus. Rather than carrying fashion footwear, the partners preferred a stable, staid business of high quality, conservative shoes. But after more than a quarter-century as partners, John W. and Carl Wallin often found themselves at odds over how to run the business.

In 1928, John W. convinced his two eldest sons, 25-year-old Everett and 24-year-old Elmer, into buying his interest in the company for about $30,000 each. ($523,000 in today's dollars.) Both graduates of the University of Washington, Everett and Elmer had been working in various capacities within the company since they were 12 years old, establishing a precedent that would be followed by members of each subsequent generation. At their father's request, they each had worked briefly for other footwear companies, which gave them a broader understanding of the industry. They both enjoyed the retail business and believed the store had great potential. In 1929, an initially reticent Wallin sold his share to the brothers. (John. W.'s youngest son, Lloyd, who was still an undergraduate at the University of Washington, would eventually join Everett and Elmer.)

In 1930, they renovated their Second Avenue store, tripling the display and merchandising area by taking over the adjoining retail space. The grand opening, August 19, 1930, marked the change of the name of the store to "Nordstrom's." The official name would eventually become "Nordstrom."

Everett, Elmer and Lloyd lived and identified with the values and principles that would eventually become known as *The Nordstrom Way*. Each succeeding generation has put their stamp on how their namesake company conducts itself both as a for-profit enterprise and a good citizen of their community.

FLEXIBILITY AND HUMILITY

AN ESSENTIAL ASPECT OF THE NORDSTROM culture is the personal humility of people named Nordstrom. As Bruce has said many times, as shoe salesmen, "We were raised on our hands and knees waiting on the customer. I consider that a literal and symbolic way of how we run our business."

Humility includes recognizing you don't know all the answers (nor should you have to), which creates a culture that's sufficiently flexible to change when change is essential to survival.

Flexibility for the greater good was established early on by Everett, Elmer and Lloyd, who knew their ability to work well together was crucial to the success of the business. Everett and Lloyd merchandised women's shoes, which represented the largest part of the business, while Elmer handled men's and children's shoes. They enjoyed the friendly, fraternal competition, and each wanted to be successful in his own area of the business. "We wanted to be the best that we could," recalled Elmer. "We had no prizes, and we didn't boast about it, but we always knew which brother was doing the best. Knowing that only made the other two try harder."

In addition to their merchandising duties, Everett oversaw finances, Elmer handled store operations and union negotiations, and Lloyd was in charge of publicity.

Decision-by-consensus leadership

As the eldest son, Everett could have claimed the title of president and relegated his brothers to support positions. (Remember, John W. had to leave Sweden because of his frustration with his elder brother.) But as Elmer recalled in his memoir *A Winning Team*, "Everett insisted on a different plan. He said, 'I'll agree to be president for now, but only if we agree to rotate the titles.' We would work our way up to president, then drop down to secretary/treasurer for two years. Then we would serve as vice-president for two years, until we became president again. People would ask us our titles and we sometimes had trouble remembering who was who on that day." The only time the brothers paid attention to their job titles was when they needed to sign business documents. Official corporate titles didn't become a legal requirement until the company was incorporated in 1938.

If Everett had not been so flexible, and had not trusted and respected his brothers, the other two might have left the store to pursue their own business interests.

Everett, Elmer and Lloyd established a "decision-by-consensus" leadership approach that could only work if all parties were flexible and trusting. That path would be successfully followed by their sons and grandsons. Their relationship was akin to a marriage. "You worked together for a common goal, but you didn't get your own way all the time," wrote Elmer. Options were discussed, argued, and challenged behind closed doors. Once a decision was made public, it was unanimous. End of discussion. That approach is foundational to The Nordstrom Way.

The brothers agreed that anything related to the business was not going to be the subject of a debate within the larger family. They didn't want any pettiness to creep into business decisions. For example, on Saturdays during college football season, they would flip a coin to see who would be free to attend their beloved University of Washington Huskies' home games because one of them had to be minding the store. Flexibility.

Perhaps the Nordstrom brothers' greatest strength was that, by all reports, they genuinely liked each other and got along well, and just as important, so did their wives. The brothers worked side by side in an office so tiny that their desks were squeezed together like a size eleven foot in a size ten shoe.

"As I watched how closely they worked together, it was fascinating to observe how they would defer to each other on their respective specialties," said Bruce (Everett's son). "They formulated strategies and reached conclusions because they were on the same wavelength and the same page. They had 100 percent respect for each other. If you're going to run a business by committee, that's absolutely necessary."

One noteworthy example came in the early 1960s when Lloyd wanted Nordstrom to expand its product offering beyond footwear by acquiring Best's Apparel, Inc., a fashionable downtown Seattle women's wear retailer that operated a second store in downtown Portland, Oregon. When Lloyd discussed the terms of the deal with his brothers, Elmer initially dissented. The middle brother thought that rather than move into the apparel business (which they did not know), the company should stick with footwear and expand to other major West Coast markets.

Lloyd, who had been negotiating the Best's Apparel deal for four years, said, "Fine. We won't do it."

That response took Elmer by surprise. "Wait a minute," he replied. "If you guys want to do it then we'll do it."

Elmer's son Jim, who attended that meeting, recalled that it made a big impression on him. "They got into a heckuva argument, deferring to each other, trying to honor the other guys' wishes. I thought that was a good lesson for my generation."

The Nordstrom brothers were disrupters.

FINANCIAL FLEXIBILITY

STARTUPS MUST BE FINANCIALLY FLEXIBLE. You never know what challenges the world presents—from economic downturns to global pandemics.

When Everett and Elmer bought the company from their father it comprised a couple of shoe stores, employing about a dozen clerks. They owned the company only on paper. John W. had loaned them some money and co-signed a bank note, which provided them with some working capital.

Then came the Great Depression, beginning in 1929, which devastated Seattle as much as it did the rest of the country. Population growth was infinitesimal. The collapse of the U.S. building trades overwhelmed the lumber-dependent Pacific Northwest region. Businesses failed, layoffs were rampant and those lucky enough to keep their jobs almost certainly took pay cuts. By 1932, the City of Seattle was bankrupt. Seattle and cities across the country saw the rise of shanty towns that drew homeless, out-of-work citizens. They were called "Hoovervilles," named after Herbert Hoover who was President of the United States during the inception of the Depression and was widely blamed for it.

Consumer buying power was stifled because fewer people were working. Wholesale and retail prices kept falling. Nordstrom's sales were way down. With customers holding on to what little money they had, the Nordstrom brothers had to sell twice as many shoes just to break even. In Seattle, people chose to resole their shoes rather than buy new ones.

"Everett and I felt that if the time ever came that my father's interests were jeopardized, we would close, liquidate the business and get out, to protect him," Elmer would later recall. One night, after closing time, the brothers locked the door of the downtown store and turned out the lights. With the only light coming from a streetlamp, they talked for several hours about the future and decided to give it another month's try. "The next month picked up a little bit and we were off to the races. But if it hadn't picked up, we would have closed up that month and there wouldn't have been a Nordstrom."

In 1937, with the country still mired in the Depression, the brothers demonstrated their commitment to their business and the future of Seattle by building a new store closer to the center of downtown retail. With that store's success, they expanded into the building next door. Although that gutsy move strapped them for cash, they were undeterred in their commitment to achieve their first big goal: to be the largest shoe store in town. They were disrupters.

"At first, the manufacturers weren't that impressed with us," wrote Elmer. "But gradually they began to favor us because they could sense we were aggressive and would probably be a good account after the war."

Should we move across the street?

Nordstrom's cultural values of flexibility and mutual respect were tested in the mid-1990s when the Nordstrom family was asked to save downtown Seattle's retail core. In 1992, after 102 years in business, the Frederick & Nelson department store closed its doors. Seattle's grand dame had been the retail anchor of downtown ever since it moved to the corner of Pine Street and Fifth Avenue in 1918.

Frederick's (as the locals called it) was similar to Marshall Field, the famed Chicago department store that acquired Frederick's in 1929. The official 100-year corporate history of Frederick's was aptly titled, "More Than a Store" because it was the place where parents took their children to get their Christmas photo sitting on Santa's lap, and where citizens bought war bonds during WWII. It was in the candy kitchen on the 9th floor where the famed Frango mint chocolate candy was created, and later shared with Marshall Field. Frederick's was a classy, well-run store famed for its outstanding customer service, a trait that had a big influence on the Nordstrom family, both personally and professionally.

"I was raised doing my back-to-school shopping with my mother at Frederick's," said Bruce. "That building had a very important place in our hearts."

Suddenly, there was an 850,000-square-foot black-eye in downtown Seattle's retail core. The abandoned Frederick's property "was disintegrating before our eyes," said Bruce. The facade was filthy, trash filled the doorways, graffiti was everywhere, and homeless people were sleeping in front of the best retail location in town.

At the same time, Nordstrom was evaluating its future in downtown Seattle. The company's existing flagship store, across the street from Frederick's, was a cobbled together, inefficient 245,000-square-foot grouping of three different buildings. Looking to the future, Nordstrom knew they must have a flagship store that reflected its image of understated elegance and operational excellence.

There was much internal discussion among the third generation of leadership. Jim felt strongly that if downtown Seattle continued to deteriorate, the company should explore moving their whole operation across Lake Washington to tony Bellevue, which was becoming Seattle's twin city.

If Nordstrom opted to remain in downtown Seattle, moving into the Frederick's building was the clear choice.

Easier said than done. There were several negatives, not least of which would be the estimated price tag of $150 million ($273 million in today's dollars) to renovate a building that was erected in 1918 and expanded in 1952. Nordstrom could have used those dollars to build stores in suburban malls in other markets.

One of the biggest negatives was the fact that several years earlier the City of Seattle blocked off one block of Pine Street—from Fourth Avenue to Fifth Avenue, where Frederick's was located—to create an urban park of sorts. As a result, shoppers driving west on Pine Street were diverted off Pine and away from the retail core.

According to Bruce, while he, Jim and Jack McMillan were willing to go along with keeping the street closed, John N. dissented in the strongest possible terms.

"My cousin John was a bulldog on that subject," said Bruce. "He had researched every single city that had closed streets to vehicular traffic—including Tacoma, Fresno, Sacramento—and found that every single one of the retail centers had died. John felt so strongly that this was such a gamble for us, we couldn't leave any stone unturned to get the best possible conditions and terms."

Nordstrom's initial public position was that keeping Pine Street closed to car traffic was a deal breaker.

Eventually the citizens of Seattle voted in a special election to approve the opening up of Pine Street to vehicular traffic by a margin of 61 percent to 39 percent. Nordstrom went ahead with its renovation plans. The company created an impressive urban retail space that opened in 1998 and sparked a retail renaissance in downtown Seattle.

As much as the flagship store is a symbol of progress, it also serves as a notice of how retail success is not forever.

"A lot of old department stores stopped changing and evolving," said Jamie, a fourth-generation company leader. "This building that once housed Frederick & Nelson is a good reminder of what happens when you don't evolve. The minute you stop evolving, the customer is going to move on."

Most long-time companies eventually fail because older executives shun risk, which means not being agile and flexible.

Changing of the Guard

Founder John W. had retired at 58 to give his sons their chance. By the late 1960s, after almost 40 years at the helm, Everett, Elmer and Lloyd were looking to exit the business, which at the time was generating about $40 million in annual sales (about $300 million in today's dollars). The store comprised most of their net worth. They each owned a third and drew the same salary every year. After they retired, they would no longer draw income from the company. Nordstrom was a private company that didn't declare dividends because that money was traditionally earmarked for expansion. The brothers needed an estate for their children who did not participate in the company. They had to find a way to generate some liquidity.

They were keenly aware of the fact that most companies eventually fail because older executives tend to shun risk, which means not being agile and flexible. That defensive, "play-it-safe" and "not-invented-here" attitude is the last stop before failure. "Employees won't find much incentive for coming up with new ideas if they know they'll be viewed by an older, conservative boss," wrote Elmer. "The result is sometimes an old taskmaster, surrounded by 'Yes-Men' rather than people who want to take charge and produce."

At the time, Everett's son Bruce, and Elmer's sons John N. and Jim, then in their thirties, had been working for Nordstrom since they were small boys and continued to sell shoes throughout high school, college and after graduation. Trained on the sales floor, the third generation was literally and figuratively, "raised kneeling in front of the customer," said Bruce. Actually, they toiled for years in the stockroom before their fathers "ever allowed us near a foot." They all went on to gain experience as buyers, department managers, and store managers. The third generation was later joined by Lloyd's son-in-law John "Jack" McMillan (husband of Lloyd's daughter Loyal), who started working for the store while an undergraduate at the University of Washington, which is the alma mater of many Nordstroms, including Everett, Elmer, Lloyd, Bruce, John N., and Jim, and the fourth generation of Blake, Pete, and Erik.

The second generation told their sons that they were considering three options:

- Selling out to another retailer

- Selling to the third generation, similar to what their fathers had done with them

- Taking the company public

Selling to the third generation was not financially feasible. Nordstrom had grown too big for their sons to afford a buyout. Although they could have borrowed the money, the debt would have strapped them for many years, which would have stymied their ambitious plans for growing the business.

Of greater significance, Everett, Elmer and Lloyd were not sold on whether Bruce, John N., Jim, and Jack could successfully duplicate their decision-by-consensus approach because, according to Jim, "We went through a period where the four of us were pointing fingers at each other. Our fathers immediately put the company up for sale. Talk about a lesson."

Once the industry heard that Nordstrom was on the selling block, many major retail giants such as Macy's expressed interest. The principal suitor was Southern California's Broadway-Hale (which was later called Carter Hawley Hale, then Broadway Stores). They offered Nordstrom a million shares of stock in Broadway-Hale, valued at about $24 a share.

As Jim told me, "When we explained to Edward Carter [chairman of Broadway-Hale Stores] how we ran our business in a decentralized way, he said, 'You can't run a business that way.' We knew we would be canned immediately after the transaction."

Furthermore, Bruce, John N., Jim and Jack were not impressed with the Broadway Hale operation, particularly its customer service. They believed that there was a huge hole in retailing that they could fill, particularly with Nordstrom's superior culture of customer service.

"Our grandpa got credit for starting the company. His three sons built it into a very viable business," said Bruce. "My generation had a chance to take it even further, to become a national company, and to leave it better than we found it, just as the previous generation had done."

The third generation devised a business plan that called for paying their fathers by issuing stock and taking the company public, with a pro forma projection of $500 million in sales in five years. Bruce, John N., Jim and Jack were shocked when the brothers accepted their offer.

"A year or two later, I asked my uncle Everett why they went along with the deal," recalled Jim. "He said, 'Because for the first time, you were all getting along, pulling in the same direction as a team, and we thought maybe you guys could do it.'"

This decision prompted Edward Carter, Chairman of Broadway Hale, to fly to Seattle to try to have the decision reversed. He told Bruce, John N., Jim and Jack that they were making a huge mistake. After all, he said, *they* would be the biggest shareholders in Broadway Hale, and in his opinion, "The price of Nordstrom stock will never equal our stock."

Carter had no idea how wrong he would be.

Broadway-Hale survived takeover attempts in 1984 and 1986, as well as a Chapter 11 bankruptcy filing in 1991. Running out of hard assets and credit to pay off suppliers, the company sold itself to Federated Department Stores in 1995. Federated is long gone. And so it goes.

A NEW GENERATION OF LEADERSHIP

AFTER THE INITIAL PUBLIC OFFERING, Everett, Elmer and Lloyd took 20 percent for themselves, which they split three ways and left the remaining 80 percent to the company.

They were concerned about who was going to be the boss among the third generation. When the second generation stepped back from the company, they selected Bruce, the eldest, to be president.

"One day," Bruce recalled, "My cousin John, who is three years younger than me, said, 'I don't know if I want to work for you my whole life.' I said, 'I respect that 100 percent. I don't want to be your boss for your whole life.'"

Jim (John N.'s younger brother) agreed. "We don't expect

brothers to work for brothers, cousins to work for cousins. My brother wouldn't work for me for a minute. I wouldn't work for him. He and Bruce wouldn't want to work for either one of us. So, we really didn't have any other option."

Bruce told his father and uncles that he and his cousins wanted to be equal. The company was considerably bigger and there was plenty to do. While the brothers had their reservations, "I had none," recalled Bruce. "I was confident that we could be successful. I told my father and my uncles, 'Either we do this thing together, or we're not going to do it.' My best argument was, 'We want to do it the way you did.'"

In May 1970, Bruce, 37; John N., 34; Jim, 31; and Jack McMillan, 39, took the helm. Elmer, Everett, and Lloyd became co-chairmen of the board. The newly created Office of the President made each young Nordstrom a co-president, with different responsibilities (which they were already doing) and each drew the same salary. They were following the same flexible power-sharing formula by which Nordstrom is still run today.

And they were told by their fathers in no uncertain terms that they were on their own—sink or swim.

"We offered encouragement and resisted the temptation to give advice," wrote Elmer. As the torch was passed, the brothers emphasized to their sons the need for constant diligence. "From our experience during the World War II years, we saw how easily a business could fall apart from neglect." They gave the younger generation a long list of potential excuses, including the weather, the economy, and the new shopping center down the block. "We told them they might as well give us their excuses by the number, because they didn't mean a thing. If business was bad, there was nowhere to put the blame but upon themselves."

Now that's the mentality of a startup.

DECISION-BY-CONSENSUS

LIKE THEIR FATHERS, THE THIRD GENERATION followed the decision-by-consensus approach. Sharing leadership is impossible without flexibility, the sublimation of ego, and the commitment to keep private disagreements unknown to those outside the inner circle.

"In any major decision—in fact any minor decision—we made in this company, if we couldn't get the family to sign off on it, we just didn't do it," said Bruce. "We were probably prevented from making some errors because one person said, 'that doesn't sound right.' The others respected that one vote enough that we would say, 'Let's go in another direction.' Some people might say that arrangement causes inaction. But because of the example our fathers set, it didn't cause inaction; it caused *action*."

"Growing up," noted Erik, Bruce's youngest son, "I thought my father and his cousins agreed on everything. When I got older and worked in the business, I saw that they agreed on almost nothing. But when they made their decision public, they were as one."

Susan Brotman, a former Nordstrom executive, recalled attending weekly Monday morning meetings that afforded her an opportunity to watch the third-generation work, to see firsthand how they discussed every issue before coming to a decision. "There was such respect among them that if someone strongly felt one way or another, they would talk it through until they arrived at what they felt was the best decision for the company."

"There is a notable absence of politics at Nordstrom."
—Alfred Osborne, retired board member.

DECISION-BY-CONSENSUS REDUX

THE FOURTH GENERATION OF Blake, Pete, and Erik, "agreed we would never have a vote," on a decision, said Erik. "If you dissent, it's your job to make the case and convince the others. And if you can't, then you need to be convinced by the others. You can't stay in the middle. You can't say, 'I think you guys are wrong, but I wasn't able to convince you, but I'm only one vote.' That's not good enough."

Alfred E. Osborne, Jr., Professor and Faculty Director at the Price Center for Entrepreneurship & Innovation at UCLA's Anderson School of Management, who served on the Nordstrom board from 1987 to 2006, told me, "There is a notable absence of politics at Nordstrom. Yes, there is some at different levels, but it is far more muted than in other companies. Once you have your say on a decision, you don't try to tear it down afterward. A lot of organizations have managers who don't know when to stop and therefore create all kinds of chaos."

The fact that the Nordstrom family members could amicably settle their differences of opinion was known to Pete Rozelle, a personal friend of Lloyd, who was the legendary commissioner of the National Football League in its most formative years, from 1960 to 1989. In 1975, the Nordstrom family was part of a Seattle group that was awarded an expansion NFL franchise for a price tag of $15 million. (You read that number correctly. Yes, $15 million for the *entire* team. (That's $69 million in today's dollars.) The NFL policy was that one person had to be the majority owner. But none of the individual Seattle investors had the required $8 million-plus to fulfill that requirement. Undeterred, Lloyd convinced Commissioner Rozelle to designate the Nordstrom *family* as the owner of 51 percent of what would eventually become the Seattle Seahawks.

When I interviewed Rozelle in 1993 about that transaction, he told me, "The Nordstroms are the only family I would let be majority owners. I was particularly impressed with their togetherness. There was never any friction with their ownership. As a family, they were always on the same page."

FLEXIBILITY IN ADVERSITY

LIKE THE SECOND GENERATION, THE THIRD generation took the helm during a period of economic difficulty. At the time, The Boeing Company was by far the largest employer in the region with 104,000 workers (at a time when the population of the entire Seattle metro area was 530,000). In addition, there was the "Boeing multiplier," consisting of local businesses that helped support and supply the airplane maker with everything from parts to food services.

In the late 1960s, Boeing was hit by two major misfortunes: (1) the federal government's termination of funding for the construction of a supersonic transport plane (SST), which forced Boeing to abandon the project; and (2) decreased demand for the new 747 jumbo jet airplane. When Boeing reduced its local payroll from 104,000 to 37,200, local unemployment shot up to almost 14 percent, which was the top rate in the U.S., and the highest of any major city since the Great Depression. So many people moved out of the region there eventually appeared a billboard that read: "The last person leaving Seattle—turn out the lights."

This time is remembered by locals as "The Boeing Bust."

"We'd had this grand scheme of taking off like a rocket, but then all of a sudden we were faced with this downturn in our home base," recalled Bruce. "That made our game plan a little scarier, but it didn't dissuade us at all."

> "Our goal was to make our numbers and we did . . . by outworking the competition."

Lloyd assembled sales associates, buyers and department managers and told them to buy *more* merchandise and hire *more* people.

"As dark as that period was, we were inspired to be bold and aggressive," recalled Bruce, who with his cousins had rejuvenated Nordstrom into a young-thinking enterprise, even though the company had already been in business for more than 60 years.

"We took a page from our fathers' playbook," said Bruce. "During World War II, when shoes were being rationed and other retailers were cutting back, they forged ahead, and grew their business. We saw the Boeing downturn as a similar opportunity for us because other retailers were pulling in their horns, buying less inventory, and running fewer newspaper advertisements. We didn't believe the gloom and doom in the media; we only believed in our sales numbers and our gut. Our goal was to make our numbers and we did, not by buying less merchandise and firing more employees, but by outworking the competition."

Because at that time, Nordstrom was still just a Northwest company with just 11 stores, Lloyd and the third-generation leadership team could regularly visit stores to communicate with employees and keep up morale during a trying time.

"That one year, 1971, was probably the best we ever had," said Bruce. "We worked harder, and we came out of it in better shape. Although we saw only a modest increase of four percent, we dramatically improved our share of the market, even though it was a smaller market."

All this was happening around the time Nordstrom went public.

Just two years later, in 1973, despite the continued downturn in the Seattle market, Nordstrom again demonstrated its faith in its hometown by expanding the downtown store, which included uniting two other adjoining buildings into one big 245,000-sq.ft. flagship store. The company had budgeted $7 million for the renovation ($49 million in today's dollars) but ended spending almost twice that much in overruns. At the store opening in November, Bruce told the *Seattle Post-Intelligencer*: "We can build suburban stores forever and they will be successful. But this—by a mile—is the biggest thing we ever did."

With the opening of the newly renovated downtown store, the official name of the company changed from Nordstrom Best to Nordstrom because the Nordstrom name had been established in the apparel industry, which was exactly what the family had set out to do.

In 1973, sales exceeded $100 million for the first time, generated by 11 company stores and 32 leased shoe departments. Only five years earlier, sales were $40 million.

In 1975, in the lower level of the flagship store, the company opened the first Nordstrom Rack discount clearance center for full-line merchandise.

The pro forma proposal put together by the third generation estimated that Nordstrom would reach $100 million in sales by 1980. As it turned out, they underestimated that number by almost $400 million.

"Our generation was very lucky," said John N. "We came into the business at the most opportune time ever in retail. Those were golden days. Customer service was our top priority."

COVID-19: The Ultimate Test of Flexibility

Despite Nordstrom's legacy of flexibility in dealing with crises of many varieties, no generation had ever faced the uncertainty of the COVID-19 pandemic. With no institutional playbook to draw from, how could the fourth generation make decisions on inventory, finances, employee and customer safety, and a myriad of other challenges both known and yet-to-be known?

Flexibility had to be the order of the day. At the same time, leadership worked to maintain the tenets of the company's century-old culture. In this volatile public health, social, and economic environment, it was imperative to be agile and communicative as well. Leadership focused on making sure they had scenarios where they could adapt on the fly. But it was, "also ensuring that we live by the values of the company as well and deliver a great customer experience," said Anne Bramman, who at the time was Chief Financial Officer.

When COVID hit in March 2020, Nordstrom closed all of its then-357 stores and furloughed a portion of its corporate employee base for what was expected to be a period of six-weeks. (Ultimately it was for three months.) All hiring was frozen. Regions were restructured; support roles were redefined for greater speed and flexibility. Eligible employees continued to receive full benefits. The board of directors received no cash payments, the executive team took temporary pay cuts, and Pete and Erik declined their salary through September 2020.

The company suspended quarterly cash dividends and share repurchases. At the height of the pandemic, Nordstrom lost its investment-grade rating and was forced to pledge inventory and assets as collateral on its credit line and to meet strict financial metrics that limited its flexibility. Operating expenses, capital expenditures, and working capital were reduced more than $500 million. Many orders for merchandise were cancelled; store lease terms were amended to give Nordstrom greater financial protection. Additional covenants restricted Nordstrom's options for financing future payments to vendors and precluded share repurchases and dividend payments until the ratings improved, which contributed to the urgency of debt refinancing in 2021.

On a call with stock analysts, Erik and then-CFO Bramman used the word "flexibility" a half-dozen times. By the first quarter of 2021, Nordstrom was in the positive position of beginning to dig out of its financial hole and put itself back on solid footing.

> One of the bedrocks of Nordstrom is the mantra "Here to Win" . . . by supporting and challenging one another to be better every day.

Channel Flexibility

Even with the prolonged closure of 357 brick-and-mortar stores, Nordstrom was in a better position than most of its competitors to handle this unprecedented situation because it had long employed an omnichannel selling strategy. Over the two decades leading up to the pandemic, Nordstrom had invested heavily in technology and hiring tech-focused employees. Nordstrom.com had been doing business and continually adding features and sophistication since 1998. The company constantly enhanced its mobile shopping apps.

During the shutdown, the biggest challenge was how to get the orders to the customers. Nordstrom had long ago invested in an easy-to-access company-wide inventory system across all channels. Distribution and fulfillment centers, as well as a small team of store fulfillment, remained open (where permitted by local authorities).

One of the bedrocks of Nordstrom is the mantra "Here to Win", which, according to company literature means, "We win as a team by supporting and challenging one another to be better every day." And that's exactly what happened. Teams pulled together from across the company to decrease inventory levels by more than 25 percent from the previous year, which enabled the company to bring in new product in season. (A fashion retailer must have new fashion. Fashion is like fresh fruits and vegetables; it's perishable.) That was no small task. Leveraging its treasure trove of data insights, the company had a handle on inventory, pricing, and reordering aligned with how customers were shopping during this period of uncertainty.

By 2023, Nordstrom set a goal of selling through its inventory at a rate 10 percent faster than 2022. The goal was to give the company the opportunity to bring in fresh merchandise from frequently. As Pete told *The Wall Street Journal*, "We want our customers to say, 'Every time I come to Nordstrom there is something new.'"

A FAILED EXPERIMENT

LOOKING FOR GROWTH IN THE BEGINNING of the 21st Century, Nordstrom cast its eye to the Canadian market, which projected to be an ideal source of expansion. Nordstrom always knew it would do well in Vancouver, British Columbia, 141 miles from Seattle. But it was not financially feasible to have just one store in Canada, because of logistic and marketing issues such as the complexity and costs of bringing merchandise across the border.

Unlike the suburban U.S. retail market, which is mall-based, Canada is more urban in its most populous markets. To create enough leverage and scale, Nordstrom opted to open one store in each of four cities: Calgary, Ottawa, Toronto and Vancouver, sufficiently spacing out the openings so that they could learn as they went along. In September 2014, Nordstrom opened its first Canada store at Chinook Centre in Calgary. In 2015, 2016, and 2017 respectively the company opened full-line stores in Ottawa, Vancouver and Toronto. Nordstrom Rack stores made their Canadian debut in 2018.

The company created some specific non-buying roles that supported merchandise divisions and helped communicate to buying teams the specific needs of Canadian consumers and helped the Canadian employees understand how Nordstrom ran its departments.

Nordstrom transformed the way it hired and trained new people. With the exception of British Columbians, most Canadians had never shopped at a Nordstrom and were not familiar with the company. Consequently, Nordstrom had to break its traditional approach of promoting from within. Newly-hired native Canadian employees were brought to Seattle for a week to learn the Nordstrom way.

"That was the most practical way for us to give them some sense of what we're aspiring to do but also to see if it fit for them," said Chris Wanlass, Vice President and General Manager, New York City, an American who was the initial manager of the Vancouver store. "We were asking them to do things they had never done before, even if they had previously worked in retail."

Alas, despite Nordstrom's best efforts, the Canadian stores failed to attract enough customers to generate profitability.

The sole exception was the store in Vancouver, which ranked near the top of all of Nordstrom's full-line stores. The Canadian media speculated on the reasons for Nordstrom's lack of success: stagnant sales growth, unfavorable exchange rates, higher economic costs, too many stores; too few stores; the Internet, high interest rates and COVID 19. In March 2023, the company announced it would be closing all six department stores and seven Nordstrom Rack stores in the country.

Nordstrom followed other U.S.-based retailers who couldn't crack the Canadian market. For example, in 2013 Target opened 133 stores north of the border, only to close them all two years later.

Flexibility requires being ready to change course when circumstances shift and/or the hypothesis of your strategy is obviously not working. Nordstrom adjusted to that reality.

"We entered Canada in 2014 with a plan to build and sustain a long-term business there. Despite our best efforts, we do not see a realistic path to profitability for the Canadian business," said Erik in a prepared statement. "We regularly review every aspect of our business to make sure that we are set up for success."

Nordstrom made another difficult decision in Spring 2023, when it announced it was closing its five-floor, 312,000 sq. ft. full-line store on Market Street in downtown San Francisco, and its 40,000 sq. ft. Rack store across the street. The flagship store at Westfield San Francisco Centre in the Union Square neighborhood opened in1988; the Rack store had been in operation since 2014. Five weeks after Nordstrom announced the closing, Westfield declared it had relinquished control of the center to its lenders,

"The dynamics of the downtown San Francisco market have changed dramatically over the past several years, impacting customer foot traffic to our stores and our ability to operate successfully," said Jamie.

Those changing dynamics included a pandemic-related shift to remote work, waning tourism, increased theft, and unsafe conditions for customers, retailers, and employees.

Nordstrom's decision to leave downtown San Francisco was shared by Whole Foods, Banana Republic, Gap, Marshall's, Anthropologie, and Office Depot.

THE MANHATTAN PROJECT

LIKE ANY STARTUP, NORDSTROM IS ALWAYS challenging itself. For example, leadership recognized that it would never be considered the finest company of its kind in the world until they had a meaningful presence in mid-town Manhattan.

After more than two decades of searching for the right location, Nordstrom opened in September 2019 on seven-levels on 57th Street and Broadway, near the corpses of former leading retailers Bonwit Teller, Henri Bendel and Barneys. Today, on the island of Manhattan, Nordstrom's prominence approaches the likes of long-time New York retail institutions Bloomingdales and Saks Fifth Avenue.

"That building is a culmination of efforts and experiences," said Bruce of the third generation. "All the accomplishments, all the times you stubbed your toe. It's sobering and humbling for a guy like me who's been here a long time." Asked how he felt about the reality that Nordstrom may be the last upscale department store standing, Bruce answered, "It's like we're running on hot coals. You have to keep moving."

As Bruce's son Erik noted, "To have a place in Manhattan is a dream come true. We challenged ourselves. It's a different standard than for other stores It couldn't be just a great Nordstrom store; it had to be one of the greatest stores in the world. Every square foot has to be great. The Manhattan store is a tangible example of how we had to bring our aspirations to life."

In 2023, coinciding with the annual National Retail Federation's Big Show in New York, Daniel Hodges, CEO of Retail Store Tours, included Nordstrom in the 10 must-see New York City stores that highlight innovations driving the future of retail. Nordstrom, Hodges wrote, "is a store where every square inch and every smile create an experience that holds attention and makes time stand still. Nordstrom is the epitome of best practices, from merchandising and dining experiences to product display and the sumptuous beauty section on the second floor. Every square inch of the store and every helpful engagement with a well-trained and motivated team member makes shoppers feel like family."

Chris Wanlass, who began his Nordstrom career in 1992, was put in charge of opening the Manhattan store. His challenge was how to take the best of his company's culture to the Big Apple and put a localized spin on it.

Although the New York leadership team was drawn from veteran Nordstrom employees, many others had non-Nordstrom pedigrees.

"We wanted to make hiring a great experience," said Wanlass. "If we make it a great place to work it'll be a great place to shop. Hiring people for the New York store, from the minute they took the elevator up to the meeting room, we wanted their first view of Nordstrom to be positive: the greeting, the waiting room, what they saw on the walls, the interview space, the interview process, the way department managers assembled their teams. We sweated all the details. We wanted to make sure we were building a diverse team."

Erik noted, "We can see the impact from the people we attract to work for Nordstrom. We are consistently surprised at the high level of talent of people who want to join our team. A lot of times it's not for a bigger job. They say it's for the brand and what it stands for."

This approach will be discussed in detail in the chapter on Social Responsibility.

> An organization can transform itself only when it wants to transform itself. It must be flexible.

"You don't have to be from Nordstrom to be good at Nordstrom"

One of the traditional bedrocks of Nordstrom was that the only path to the top began on the sales floor, especially if your last name is Nordstrom. In recent years, the company has recruited talented outsiders who share the company philosophy of putting the customer first.

"Our organization is like an organism," said Pete. "When a foreign body comes in, the organism wants to reject it. But if someone new comes to the team and makes us better, they get accepted real fast. A great teaching point for me is that you don't have to be from Nordstrom to be good at Nordstrom."

Olivia Kim, who in 2012 was vice president of creative at the avant-garde emporium Opening Ceremony in New York, had a growing reputation within the fashion world for partnering with famous brands and creating attention-grabbing projects. Meeting Pete in 2012, Kim recalled, "I was so taken aback by this guy. Instead of boasting about himself or his company, he talked about all the things they were looking for in places where they felt they needed to get ahead, or places where they were underserved."

An organization can transform itself only when it wants to transform itself. It must be flexible.

Pete offered Kim a job. "Doing what?," she asked. To which he replied: "I don't know."

For Kim, "To have access to a big company but to have an entrepreneurial, scrappy project within the walls of that just felt really exciting for me. We figured it out together. Pete just kind of said, 'Here are the keys to the car; you drive.'"

Kim was hired in 2013 as Vice President of creative projects, in charge of pop-up shops, brand collaborations, and exclusives with digitally native brands. She has lured new customers by making Nordstrom a destination for fashion inspiration and brands that can't be easily found elsewhere.

"Pete has that curiosity of what's outside our company and having humility," said Erik. "As much as we believe in our culture, having worked on the salesfloor, we know that there are people with other experiences that can help us. They totally get what Nordstrom is about. That was a good lesson for me. Our culture is not that tricky. It's not hard for people with the same sensibilities and values to join us and be all in pretty quickly. Olivia and Sam Lobban [British-born executive vice president, general merchandising manager for men's and women's apparel and all designer areas] both get it. They have experiences that we don't have. You make the team better by adding diversity and the talent you don't have."

Takeaways

- Bet on yourself

- Challenge yourself to work outside your comfort zone

- No job is too small

- Do whatever it takes

- There's flexibility in humility

- Recognize you don't have all the answers

- Teamwork—use all available resources to make transactions seamless

- Financial flexibility helps to survive emergencies

- Flexibility means being open to new ideas

- No excuses for subpar performance

- Be bold and aggressive

- Flexibility promotes learning

AGILITY

physical or mental dexterity

A

Agility is the ability to adapt and respond to change. Agile organizations view change as an opportunity, not a threat.

— **Jim Highsmith,** coauthor of *The Agile Manifesto*

As they aggressively expanded their business in the 1940s, Elmer, Everett and Lloyd built relationships with shoe company sales representatives by treating them with kindness and hospitality.

"I fondly recall the countless times when my dad brought home traveling salesmen and manufacturer's representatives for dinner and drinks," said Bruce. "If we'd had a larger house, we probably would have let them sleep there. We got to know these salesmen well. My sister Anne and I looked forward to one particular salesman coming to our house because he always brought us big all-day lollipops."

Not surprisingly, when a salesman found himself with extra pairs to sell, he often offered them first to the Nordstroms.

Those relationships came in handy with the onset of the Second World War. Merchandise was scarce because much of the leather supply and domestic footwear production was earmarked for military use. Manufacturers were expected to reserve one-half of their production for the war effort. Prices were frozen. Retailers were given a cutoff date, after which all prices had to remain in effect for the war's duration which was, of course, unknown.

Citizens were issued quota ration stamps for practically every consumer product, from meat to shoes. Because shoe retailers were assigned a certain number of pairs they could sell, they routinely doubled their usual orders in order to ensure delivery of half of what they needed. Once they met their daily quota, many stores closed up shop, even in the middle of the day. The Nordstrom brothers did the opposite. By prepaying their suppliers, they were able to get deliveries when competitors couldn't.

> "When people think they can't buy something, they want it even more."

"We could sell as many shoes as we could get," Elmer wrote in *The Winning Team*. "The trouble was getting them." To make sure they had plenty of merchandise to sell, the Nordstrom brothers traveled right to the source. Elmer got on a train to Milwaukee, Wisconsin, then the heart of men's shoe manufacturing. Everett and Lloyd traveled to St. Louis, Missouri, the hub of women's and children's shoes.

"They camped on the doorsteps of those manufacturers and got to know them on a personal level," said Elmer's son John N. "We got product when our competitors couldn't. They don't teach you that in business school."

Consequently, Nordstrom earned a reputation for being the store that had the shoes. That's how they drew customer traffic. Because there were so many people lined up waiting to get into the store, the fire department would allow in only a certain number of people at any one time. (Similar to reopening stores during COVID-19.) Bruce, who was a young child at the time, recalled, "Customers would literally buy everything we had. Never has business been so easy. When people think they can't buy something, they want it even more—whether they need it or not." By the time the war was over in 1945, Nordstrom had become a nationally recognized shoe power, famous for aggressive buys and vast inventories, and was well on its way to becoming the largest independent shoe chain in the United States, with eight locations in Washington and Oregon.

Nordstrom also repaired shoes. One notable customer in need was a visitor from Memphis, Tennessee, named Elvis Presley, who was in Seattle in 1962 to film "Meet Me at the World's Fair" (which was taking place in Seattle). One afternoon, Colonel Tom Parker, the entertainer's manager, came running into the store carrying a pair of pointed boots that had split open on the sides. The colonel told Elmer that Elvis was across the street in his stocking feet, surrounded by excited female fans.

"We took them down to our shoe repair department and gave them V.I.P. treatment," Elmer recalled. "You couldn't have the King of Rock'n'Roll walking around outside Nordstrom's without a pair of shoes."

GIVE ME AGILITY OR GIVE ME DEATH

I HAVE TAUGHT AN ELECTIVE CLASS to marketing majors at Western Washington University, located where I live in Bellingham, Washington, entitled, "Retail Reinvention: Everything Old is New Again." I ask students to research once-dominant retailers that either no longer exist or are decidedly diminished. It's a virtually endless list that includes the A&P supermarket chain, Borders Books, Blockbuster Video, and Thom McCan Shoes, to name just a few.

I ask the students two simple questions that invariably lead to the same answers:

1. **Why did these companies succeed?**
   Answer: They were innovative and filled a need in the marketplace.

2. **Why did these companies eventually fail?**
   Answer: They weren't agile enough to adapt to change.

"Enjoying success requires the ability to adapt," said Nolan Ryan, the Hall of Fame baseball pitcher who was wildly erratic in his early years before he changed his delivery. "Only by being open to change will you have a true opportunity to get the most from your talent."

As I wrote this book in 2022 and 2023, the retail sector continued to be buffeted by the proverbial winds of change. For examples, look no further than Bed Bath & Beyond, Starbucks and Amazon.

Like every merchant that has operated in every marketplace, Bed Bath & Beyond and Starbucks (both launched in 1971) reached a point where they were forced to re-evaluate their reasons for being.

Bed Bath & Beyond was slow to modernize their stores and their supply chain. By the beginning of 2023, the firm closed 150 stores and received a cash injection of $1 billion to temporarily put off bankruptcy until April when the retailer announced it was going out of business. In a 2023 interview with *The Wall Street Journal*, co-founder Warren Eisenberg admitted that he and co-founder Leonard Feinstein were slow to adapt to the rise of e-commerce: "We missed the boat on the internet." Feinstein also conceded that he and Eisenberg should have ceded power much earlier to younger managers. "I don't know if you should be running a big business when you're in your 80s."

In mid-2023, Overstock.com acquired certain intellectual-property assets of Bed Bath & Beyond for $21.5 million and rebranded itself as Bedbathandbeyond.com.

Starbucks, still a successful company, has had to redefine itself and its purpose, moving to a fast-paced takeout environment, which is 180 degrees away from former CEO Howard Schultz's original concept of a relaxing, leisurely "Third Place." (The First Place is home, and the Second Place is work. For many remote workers, that's now the same place). In 2023, Starbucks—with almost 18,000 stores in the U.S.—announced plans to add nearly 400 U.S. stores offering only delivery or pickup service over the next three years. In its quarter ending Oct. 2, 2022, some 72 percent of its U.S. sales were taken to go.

"That is a complete turnaround for where it once was, which was the majority of the business was in our store," said Schultz.

Amazon's smart-device features such as Alexa have not met expectations for suggesting and promoting consumer purchases. Although Amazon's initial business was retail (beginning with books in 1995), as a mature company, it's growth had been coming from advertising, subscriptions, logistics and its Amazon Web Services' cloud-storage operations.

Brick-and-mortar stores have been more of a challenge. In 2022 and 2023, Amazon shut down all 20 of its Amazon

Books physical bookstores, as well as its Amazon 4-star and Amazon Pop Up shops, which sold a variety of electronics and other hot items. The closures affected 68 stores across the U.S. and U.K. The company put the brakes on the rollout of more Amazon Fresh stores after they failed to meet consumer expectations. Physical retail is not easy.

From the beginning, Bezos has been telling his colleagues, workforce and the world that Amazon is in "Day 1" of its journey. In fact, one of the buildings in Amazon's urban Seattle complex is called "Day 1," which reflects on how focusing on the long term leads to larger success. "Day 1" is a phrase that Bezos repeats at the end of each yearly letter to shareholders.

At an all-hands meeting several years ago, Bezos was asked what Day 2 looks like.

His answer: "Day 2 is stasis. Followed by irrelevance. Followed by excruciating, painful decline. Followed by death. And *that* is why it is *always* Day 1."

It's all about adapting to current circumstances.

"The only sustainable advantage you can have over others is agility," Bezos has said. "Because nothing else is sustainable, everything else you create, somebody else will replicate."

While many retailers (including Nordstrom) were closing physical stores for a variety of reasons, several others were opening stores. One notable example was Warby Parker, which began selling eyeglasses exclusvely online in 2010. The premise of the company was to sell directly to consumers. Because retail demands agility, Warby Parker reacted to rising costs in digital advertising for attracting new online customers by opening hundreds of stores in North America. Other formerly online-only companies have followed suit. In retail, everything old is new again.

The Courage to be Agile

In the early 1980s, when Gail Cottle became Nordstrom's corporate merchandise manager for women's junior sportswear, the business in that product category had not been good; it needed to adapt to current times in order to attract younger customers. That meant modernizing the look, feel and ambiance of the department at a time when MTV music videos helped define the era. Cottle wanted to create a new in-store environment—an open warehouse feel with TV monitors playing music videos—that was a radical departure for then-traditional Nordstrom, which typically featured live in-store pianists playing soothing pop standards, show tunes, and the like.

"I presented this idea at a store planning meeting, where you had to get the stamp of approval," recalled Cottle, who retired in 2002 as an executive vice president. "I remember the looks on their faces. None of them said very much. Bruce's arms were folded, which was not a good sign. Finally, he smiled and said, 'Okay, Gail, we're with you on a win, and we'll be with you on a draw.' The message was clear: This is a big change and a big expense. We're going to go with you on it, but it had better be good. Of course, that made you work your fanny off, like there was no tomorrow. But it worked. It helped turn around our juniors business."

Post-COVID: Reopening Stores

How do you offer a luxury shopping experience during a pandemic? How do you create a warm, inviting environment? How do you demonstrate products? How do you keep dressing rooms sanitary and safe?

Agility.

Nordstrom reopened stores in a phased, market-by-market approach where allowed by local authorities. The company conducted health screenings for employees; provided face coverings for employees and customers; took steps to allow for social distancing of six feet or more (including limiting the number of customers and employees in the store at any one time); increased cleaning and sanitization; modified the fitting room experience; continued to offer contactless curbside services at full-line stores; adjusted hours of operation; and paused or adapted high-touch services and customer buying events. For a short period of time, merchandise that had been tried-on or returned was kept off the sales floor until properly disinfected. (It was soon clear that it was impossible to perform this precaution at Nordstrom's scale of operation. Also, there was very little indication that COVID was transmitted on surfaces or clothing.)

The pandemic had its plusses, including accelerating Nordstrom's ongoing reexamination of the role of its brick-and-mortar stores. As a result, in 2020, the company shuttered 16 of its 116 full-line stores, which was the first large-scale store closing activity in its history. The crisis was an opportunity to drive change more quickly and to re-evaluate, according to Erik, "the capabilities we want, how we want to show up to customers, and the competitive advantages we can have."

Nordstrom always starts by asking the basic question: "What problem is that technology solving for the customer?"

TECHNOLOGY

THINKING LIKE A STARTUP INCLUDES KNOWING that some strategies and ideas will work, and some will fail. "Trial and error" is a phrase that's part of the DNA at Nordstrom, which has never shied away from technology.

Nordstrom portrays itself as, "Customer Obsessed and Digitally Enabled," which means embracing consumer-focused tools that make for an easier and more convenient experience for customers to shop, and easier and more lucrative for salespeople to sell more stuff. The name of the game is increased sales.

Nordstrom always starts by asking the basic question: *What problem is that technology solving for the customer?*

"For us, doing it right means viewing things through the eyes of the customer," said Erik. "We always ask ourselves, 'How is this change good for the customer?'"

In the 1930s, Nordstrom introduced some "high tech" into the store experience with the Pedoscope, a shoe-fitting fluoroscope x-ray machine. The four-foot-high metal and walnut device, in the shape of short column, featured an opening where a child or adult placed their feet, and looked through a porthole for a clear x-ray view of the bones of their feet and the outline of the shoes they were trying on, including the stitching around the edges. Two other viewing portholes on either side enabled the parent and the salesperson to observe the child's toes being wiggled to show how much room for the toes there was inside the shoe. In later years, a historian wrote that fluoroscopes proved, "as attractive and exciting to little customers as free balloons and lollipops, and they were a terrific help in fitting shoes."

More than eight decades later, Nordstrom experimented with 3-D technology from Swedish-based company Volumental to measure a shopper's most accurate shoe size. The customer stepped on a platform that resembled a square-shaped digital weight scale. Three-dimensional cameras on all four corners produced a volumetric scan of each foot that measured arch length, ball, and in-step. The 3-D scan was then displayed on a tablet, which helped shoe salespeople find the ideal fit.

Before online shopping became popular in the mid-to-late-1990s, Nordstrom experimented with several technologies intended to take shopping beyond brick-and-mortar stores. In the early 1990s, Nordstrom joined with Bloomingdale's in an hour-long closed-circuit home-shopping show, produced by the National Broadcasting Company's NBC Direct subsidiary, originating from their respective stores at Minnesota's Mall of America. (Bloomingdale's closed their store in 2012). Goods were ordered with a toll-free telephone number. Alas, results were underwhelming.

Another short-lived experiment in 1991 was Nordstrom Personal Touch America, an e-mail shopping service. At the time, it was revolutionary for a customer to communicate with a salesperson via e-mail. It was an early attempt to sell apparel on the Internet, albeit with no pictures of the items. "We leveraged the inventory in Store One [the Seattle flagship store] to fulfill orders," said retired executive Geevy Thomas, who launched the service. "We believed the Internet was the future."

The company also tried its hand with an in-flight shopping service. Nothing ventured, nothing gained.

"If you don't try new things, you'll never innovate," said Jamie." "Don't panic if something doesn't work. Celebrate it!"

AGILITY IN SHOPPING CHANNELS

IN THE EARLY 1990S, THE INTERNET'S commercial possibilities were a glint in the eye of a thirty-something New York investment banker named Jeff Bezos, who would soon locate his online bookselling company in Seattle—Nordstrom's backyard. Bezos was keenly aware of Nordstrom's focus on customer service, which was one reason why he wanted Amazon to be considered "the world's most customer-centric company."

When Amazon successfully launched its website in July of 1995, it began the most profound disruption of the retail sector in more than half a century. Amazon proved that people would make purchases online, even when the Internet was in its most primitive stages, and customers worried whether their credit cards were secure. As it turned out, books were the Trojan Horse for Amazon's entry into internet retail. Those who were paying attention to retail trends understood that Amazon had the potential to eventually reach its ultimate goal of becoming "The Everything Store."

Few legacy brick-and-mortar retailers reacted as quickly as Nordstrom, where executives who saw the future of retail and were not going to be left behind. Dan Nordstrom (Jim's oldest son; Jamie's brother), another member of the fourth generation, recognized that the Internet was a viable business channel. In order to stay competitive in this new world of retail, Nordstrom invested heavily in Information Technology. To demonstrate how serious they were, Nordstrom partnered with Benchmark Capital, a storied Silicon Valley firm that went on to finance many tech companies, including eBay, Uber and Instagram. The Benchmark partnership was Nordstrom's signal to shareholders, investors, and the industry that it was ready to compete in this new world of retail, employing technology that would ultimately improve their customer experience. In addition, Nordstrom invested in seed venture funds focused on retail-related technology so that it had a front row seat for where the industry was headed.

"We told analysts that e-commerce was the future, and customers were telling us that they liked it. Nordstrom showed a lot of flexibility and agility and openness to try something new," said the then-Chief Financial Officer Mike Koppel.

> Nordstrom has the strongest online platform among traditional brick-and-mortar retailers.

NordstromShoes.com, one of the company's first online efforts, was branded "The World's Biggest Shoe Store," taking a cue from Amazon's boast of being "The World's Biggest Book Store." NordstromShoes.com claimed to have over 20 million pairs of shoes.

The company had developed its own website in-house at a time when many retailers such as Walmart and Barnes & Noble separately managed their dot-com and brick-and-mortar businesses, with different teams and different organizations in different cities. Until 2010, there was a completely separate buying organization for the website as well as a team that oversaw various digital functions. Other retailers ignored online shopping altogether, perhaps hoping it would be a fad.

Nordstrom.com debuted for the 1998 holiday shopping season.

Agility enabled the company to respond to the changing retail landscape. Adjusting to the new reality of online sales, Nordstrom lured technology experts from Amazon and other companies who knew how to build front-end customer-oriented user interfaces and how to analyze data and statistics.

Bringing in outsiders was transformative for Nordstrom, which did not have a deep bench of tech talent.

"Nordstrom was a company where most of the people, including executives, began their careers on the salesfloor and worked their way up," recalled Koppel, the retired CFO. "Then all of a sudden, there's this channel driven by a computer on a desk, where you don't have that personal interaction. That was a big pill to swallow for a company that always thought the only way to be successful was to start out kneeling on one knee in front of the customer and learning to fit a pair of shoes."

In 2011, Nordstrom acquired HauteLook a members-only shopping website offering flash-sales and limited-time sale events featuring women's and men's fashion, jewelry and accessories, beauty products, kid's clothing and toys, and home décor. HauteLook, which had launched in 2007, gave Nordstrom the technical platform to create an online off-price business. Eventually (as planned), HauteLook was absorbed into the Nordstrom Rack off-price division, paving the way for the introduction of NordstromRack.com.

The company will rarely if ever be the first to introduce new technology. They prefer to wait and see if it works, and then they'll jump in. Employing that prudent approach, Nordstrom has built the strongest online platform among traditional brick-and-mortar department stores. In 2022, Nordstrom was selected as the Number One omnichannel retailer in the country by the online magazine *Total Retail*, which cited the company's "frictionless cross-channel shopping experiences," across a variety of categories including:

- Buy online pick up in-store (BOPIS); curbside pickup

- Search in-store products online

- Shared cart

- Loyalty points earned/redeemed across all channels

- Return products across channels

- Ship from store/Endless aisle

- Pricing consistency across channels

- In-store mobile payments

As of this writing, 40 percent of Nordstrom's sales come from the combination of Nordstrom.com and NordstromRack. com. During the height of COVID, more than 50 percent of sales were from online.

(I will be delving deeper into the marriage of digital and physical in the chapter on "Transformation.")

THE CHANGING ROLE OF SALESPEOPLE

ONE OF THE COMPANY'S CORE VALUES is encouraging every salesperson to be an "Owner at Heart." Nordstrom encourages employees to work as though it's *their* name on the door, to build *their* own personal business and do what *they* feel is right to create lasting relationships with *their* customers. That philosophy is established on the first day of orientation, when new salespeople are given a card entitled "Nordstrom Employee Handbook," which contains just one rule. (see illustration) That's empowerment.

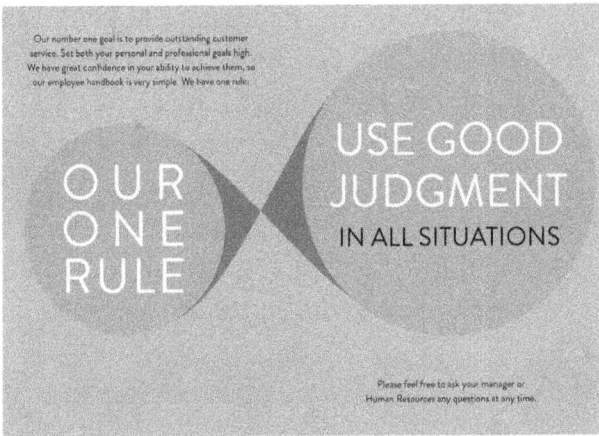

Our number one goal is to provide outstanding customer service. Set both your personal and professional goals high. We have great confidence in your ability to achieve them, so our employee handbook is very simple. We have one rule:

OUR
ONE
RULE

USE GOOD
JUDGMENT
IN ALL SITUATIONS

Please feel free to ask your manager or Human Resources any questions at any time.

Nordstrom's empowerment culture is illustrated by the company's structure of an inverted pyramid (See illustration). The inverted pyramid was born in 1971 when Nordstrom made its initial public offering of stock. At that time, a stock analyst asked the company for its organizational chart. To his surprise, none existed. John N. of the third generation recalled, "Somebody suggested that we take a pyramid and flip it upside down."

The Inverted Pyramid

CUSTOMERS

SALES & SUPPORT PEOPLE

DEPARTMENT MANAGERS

STORE MANAGERS, REGIONAL MANAGERS, CORPORATE HEADQUARTERS

EXECUTIVE TEAM, BOARD OF DIRECTORS

At the very top of the inverted pyramid are the customers. Beneath them are the salespeople, department managers, and executives, all the way down to the board of directors. This is both a literal and symbolic way of how the company does its business. The customers are obviously on top because they are the most important people in the relationship. But the *next* most important are the salespeople because they are the ones who are closest to the customers—whether in-store or digitally.

"The relationship we have with our employees is the most important relationship," said John N. "They would only believe that customer service was all important if we reinforced it every single day, which we did. It wasn't Harvard Business School stuff."

Retired company executive Betsy Sanders told me, "Nordstrom, at its best, keeps recreating the relationship with the customer. There's no script. God forbid! It's using best judgment at all times."

> "When you're nice to customers and you treat them well, they buy more from you."

THE TIRE STORY

ONE ESSENTIAL ELEMENT OF NORDSTROM'S RESPECT for customers is its liberal return policy.

"We are known for our policy that we take everything back. It boils down to the customer and how we take care of them, which is ingrained in our culture," Pete explained.

The most famous Nordstrom return story (which the national press frequently cites) is the tale of the salesperson who gladly took back a pair of automobile tires and gave the customer a refund.

What doesn't ring true?

Nordstrom has never sold tires.

Is the story apocryphal?

No. It's true! In 1975, Nordstrom acquired three stores in Alaska from the Northern Commercial Company, a full-line department store chain that sold many products, including tires. (Northern Commercial was the local B.F. Goodrich dealer.) After Nordstrom bought the stores, the company converted them to Nordstroms and eliminated lots of departments, including the tire department.

Then one day, a customer who normally spent most of his time in the Alaska wilderness, arrived at the Fairbanks store with a couple of tires that he had bought a while back in that building, just not from Nordstrom. Northern Commercial had guaranteed the tires. If the customer was not satisfied, he would be entitled to a full refund.

Craig Trounce, the Nordstrom associate who worked in the Fairbanks store in the 1970s and took back the tires, told the story on Pete's podcast, "The Nordy Pod." Trounce described the customer with the tires as a backwoods "hermit" who traveled 50 miles to make his return. Trounce called a local tire dealer to find out how much the tires were worth (about $25 each at the time) and refunded the money.

"I was congratulated by my manager who realized I had the situation under control and did the right thing," Trounce recalled.

This has become the quintessential Nordstrom return story. One hears variations of it all over the world. When I speak to corporate groups, the number one question (there is no close number two) asked is: "Is the tire story true?"

Now you know the rest of the story.

And here's the kicker: In 2022, it happened again.

As Pete aired on his podcast, one day a woman customer lugged a tire to the Nordstrom store at the upscale Americana on Brand shopping center in Glendale, California. Why did she do that? She told Mari Carrion, who worked in the customer experience department at the store, that it all started when she ordered a baby blanket from Nordstrom. But instead of delivering the baby blanket, a third-party package transport service dropped off a tire that arrived with no packaging. Taped to the tire was a slip of paper identifying Nordstrom as the shipper. The customer called Nordstrom and was asked to bring the tire to the Glendale store to process the return.

When the customer arrived with the tire, "I was surprised and excited at the same time," said Mari, who like most Nordstrom employees was well aware of the legendary tire story. "I was thinking, 'Wow, we're going back in time! This is really happening!'" Mari did not have to call Carmine Matera, the Nordstrom store manager in Glendale, for permission to accept the return. Mindful of Nordstrom's one rule: *use good judgment in all situations*, she made the decision to honor the customer by taking back the tire, simply because it was the right thing to do.

"Do the right thing" is a key tenet of the Nordstrom culture.

"We kept the tire in the store. [The shipper] never asked for it back," said Carmine Matera. "We now use the tire for telling that story, reminding everyone to say 'yes' to the customer; to stop and listen to each situation. I share that story with new hires. It keeps the culture going."

Despite the challenges inherent in Nordstrom's maintaining its liberal returns policy, "what we get [in return] is invaluable," Pete told the beauty web site *Glossier*. "There's no amount of marketing or anything you could do to engender that kind of goodwill, that kind of word-of-mouth and that kind of loyalty. When you [serve a customer well], you can see it, in terms of the way you get more wallet share from that customer. So it's a pure business strategy . . . We have found and learned over time that, when you're nice to customers and you treat them well, they buy more from you."

"It's in our DNA to take care of people."

HIGH TOUCH AND HIGH TECH:
TAKING CARE OF THE CUSTOMER

THE HISTORIC NORDSTROM APPROACH TO taking care of customers was built on high-touch, in-person transactions, often with the same salesperson, over many years. Agile salespeople are emboldened and encouraged to approach problems with curiosity and create solutions; to unlock potential, to be daring, to think big and to inspire innovation.

I love this example of creative problem solving, which came from a letter that an appreciative mom wrote to Nordstrom.

After purchasing a prom dress for her 16-year-old daughter, the mom hoped to find a pair of matching shoes for her daughter, who walked with crutches and wore braces on her feet that reached halfway up her shin. Consequently, for formal affairs, she always had to wear shoes that, in the mom's words, were "ugly and clunky."

The Nordstrom shoe saleswoman promised the mom she would find the perfect shoe for the teenager. When the mom returned to the store with her daughter, the saleswoman brought out a shoe that matched perfectly. The teenager "tried it on her like she was Cinderella," wrote the mother. "It fit!!!!!!"

The daughter, mother, and saleswoman discussed whether to have a shoemaker add a bit of "insurance" (a strap or tie) to make sure the shoe would stay on. The saleswoman suggested that if they added a strap, they could hide it with a bow. As the mother and daughter were leaving, the saleswoman asked them to return with a picture of the girl at the prom, which they did.

When customers perceive associates less as salespeople and more as problem-solvers, those associates become more powerful ambassadors for the store brand they represent.

"It's in our DNA to take care of people," said Erik. "That's the type of people we naturally attract and in crisis environments, their character comes through. We can teach the business of retailing to anyone, but we can't teach them to be personable, empathetic and engaging . . . to be just a nice person."

Every employee (whether they work on the sales floor or in a support position) is focused on making people feel good. The culture is centered on creating an environment where employees feel supported and empowered to do just that. The company has always focused on hiring and coaching salespeople who are motivated and energized to take care of their customers as they deem appropriate.

"Our business had largely worked the same way for generations," said Pete. "We don't sell anything people need. We sell things people want. We largely sell stuff that people can, if they want to put in some effort, find in other places. So there has to be a reason to have a relationship with us. Because of technology and because of our size and scale, we had to figure out how to do things differently in order to bring money to the bottom line."

> Nordstrom's end goal is unchanged:
> Enhance the experience at every touchpoint
> along the customer's buying journey.

When I wrote the original version of *The Nordstrom Way* in 1995 (the year Amazon.com was launched), the focus was on the company's in-store, high-touch approach as demonstrated by empowered people on the salesfloor who built long-lasting relationships with customers. Those salespeople knew what was in their loyal customers' closets and kept a data base of customers' tastes in brands, styles, and colors. They knew the names of customers' spouses or partners and children. They knew anniversary dates and birthdays.

There is great value for a customer who has a relationship with a professional salesperson who anticipates customers' needs and goes the extra mile, sometimes even visiting a customer's home to edit their closet. Because peoples' lives are busier and faced with greater time restraints, there's as much demand for that kind of personal relationship as there has ever been. Even if a customer doesn't set foot in a Nordstrom store, the salesperson who takes care of them can earn commission when they directly influence a customer's online purchase through an e-mail or text recommendation.

Although there have been changes in what constitutes good service and the ways that Nordstrom serves, the end goal remains the same: *Enhance the experience at every touch point along the individual customer's buying journey.*

As Bruce likes to say, "The happiest customer is the one leaving the store with a Nordstrom bag in their hand." Or having a Nordstrom package delivered to their doorstep or their place of business.

Nordstrom gives salespeople tools and access to social media to engage with customers, to create excitement about new styles, and to find something cool they didn't know they had to have. Whether using their in-store terminals or mobile point-of-sale devices, salespeople have a single view of all of

Nordstrom's inventory in their home store, as well as other full-line Nordstrom stores, Nordstrom.com, NordstromRack.com, and in distribution centers, which gives them the ability to locate and secure an item quickly for the customer. Customers can use their smartphone to scan any item, see the price, decide what size and color they want, and then have their purchases delivered to their home, place of business or hotel anywhere in the U.S.

Text messaging enables salespeople to provide their customers with a personalized styling experience. Customers who opt-in can receive from a salesperson or personal stylist private text messages that contain a description or photo of one or more items. If the customer likes any of the items recommended by the salesperson, they can make the purchase by replying "buy" and entering a unique code. Purchases are completed through the individual's Nordstrom.com account and are shipped directly using the retailer's free standard delivery.

Nordstrom's digital channel has tens of thousands of videos, running 15 to 45 seconds, where expert salespeople talk about the details of a product and demonstrate how it can be styled with other products and accessories. These videos replicate for customers the sense of discovery and confidence in their purchase. The company has a livestream shopping platform featuring salespeople and influencers, as well as virtual styling events that include curated runway pieces and a live, interactive Q&A session.

PERSONALIZATION

"THE STARS OF OUR COMPANY HAVE always been our best salespeople and personal stylists," said Erik. "Styling is our competitive advantage. We need a spectrum from low-touch to high-touch, from personal styling to digital styling. How can we adapt that to the modern world? It can't be one-to-one. It should be one-to-many and being able to leverage that. With a single salesperson, there's only so much you can do. To go from serving one to serving many, we needed to make artificial intelligence smarter. That's an example of adapting our strength in styles and people to how customers want to shop now. Customers want recommendations. They want to know how to put looks together."

To help customers with their decisions, in 2017 Nordstrom. com launched an online feature called "Looks," which shows how to take different items to put together an outfit—by style or activity. Also available on the Nordstrom app, "Looks" shows custom outfits curated by professional stylists made to match each product on the site. All items in the ensemble are viewed on the same product page. A customized "Your Looks" feature offers specific outfits based on each customer's searches, purchase history and interactions with stylists. Stylists can help a customer edit their closet; create new looks with items they already have; rediscover their favorites with alterations; and augment their wardrobe with new pieces.

> Nordstrom is continually intensifying personalization both in-store and digitally.

The Nordstrom Analytical Platform (NAP) is a real-time, event streaming–centric platform that provides insights on everything from customer services to credit. With access to a vast amount and variety of data, NAP can paint a 360° view of a customer that helps to create personalized experiences and product suggestions.

The company has invested in two platforms for mobile phones: BevyUp and MessageYes.

BevyUp's digital selling platform, which is integrated into the Nordstrom mobile employee app, extends a sales associate's relationships with their customers beyond brick-and-mortar. BevyUp's clienteling app, Style Boards, enables stylists to coordinate outfits that can be viewed digitally on a cell phone. The results are a personalized, omnichannel experience for their customers.

Nordstrom is continually intensifying personalization both in-store and digitally. During the COVID-19 reset, the company set an ambitious goal of eventually tripling its selection of stock-keeping units (inventory) from 300,000 to 1.5 million to help customers who already know what they're shopping for, and to personalize the experience for each customer.

MessageYes, a platform rooted in conversational commerce, helps customers discover and purchase brands that they want to engage with, and to transact directly with them. It also enables customers to locate their closest Nordstrom store and book an appointment with a personal shopper. Customers browse the app and select items they'd like to try on in the store. Within two hours they'll get a text that alerts them when the items have been found and that the items will be held for them until the store closes the following day. Respecting the fact that customers act differently in each channel, the app is customized to reflect the customer's experience. Message recipients simply reply "Yes" to instantly buy from their mobile phones. The platform learns from customer feedback, which makes the customer experience unique to each person and brand—personalization.

In 2023, Nordstrom added to its app a 360° augmented reality (AR) feature that enables customers to view more than

300 different men's, women's and kid's shoes in high-resolution three dimension. From every angle of the product, customers can zoom in and out to and see if it goes with items in their current wardrobe. The goal is that customers will have greater confidence in ordering the item and will be less likely to return it.

SALESPEOPLE ARE STILL IMPORTANT

THIS SENSE OF OWNERSHIP AND EMPOWERMENT is as important today as ever, but it takes additional forms and additional digital tools to engage and serve and satisfy. While sales in Nordstrom's full-line, full-price stores now represent only about one-third of all sales, the most successful salespeople are selling more than ever.

"Selling $1 million in a year is a big milestone," said Erik. In 2021, we had 75 percent more million-sellers than we did pre-pandemic and it's not because there was 75 percent more store traffic that year. Selling changed because the customer changed. The selling job isn't just serving the customer who walks into the store. It's also serving customers who are not coming into the store. They still want a real person to help them with discovery, to suggest things, to give them confidence to try something new. We need to meet the customer where they are."

> The principles of serving the customer haven't changed, but the tools are different.

"We are in the first or second inning on how to deliver on customers' increasingly high expectations," says Jamie, Chief

Merchandising Officer. "It's a never-ending cycle of listening to what the customer is asking for and getting the team to deliver on that demand. Good service is not the absence of bad service. Good service is often invisible. You don't notice it. In a top restaurant, they pour you a glass of water, you drink from it, and then your server automatically refills the water as opposed to asking if you want more water. We want to be in the place where your glass is always full."

Motivated salespeople use social media and other digital platforms to make connections with customers who live in different cities; customers whom they have never met.

Jesse James Barnholdt is the quintessential motivated Nordstrom salesperson. Based in Pittsburgh, Pennsylvania, Jesse has worked for Nordstrom on both the West Coast and East Coast since 2005. Beginning in 2015, he has used his Instagram social media platform to generate more than $2 million in annual sales, selling men's and women's shoes, women's handbags, ready-to-wear apparel and accessories.

"The big thing about social media is that you're not depending on foot traffic," said Barnholdt, who has well over 100,000 followers on his Instagram account and more than 1.2 million impressions a week. When he posts his own pictures of new product, customers interested in buying the item send him their phone number, which is answered by a Nordstrom-generated text message with a link to make the purchase. Barnholdt then sends the customer a "digital thank-you note," which tags the customer's name. The customer in turn clicks "add to the story," which lets other people learn about their new purchase.

"Not only am I thanking them, but they are also advertising for me," said Barnholdt. "All their followers see me, and I can get more customers that way. It's a snowball effect." Barnholdt's

500,000-plus annual clicks serve the purpose of driving people to Nordstrom.com. "The principles of serving the customer haven't changed, but the tools are different."

Pete noted, "No one told Jesse to do all those things. He looked at the landscape of how business is done and figured out how to use the Internet to his advantage and for the customer's advantage."

Justin Leggett, another top salesperson, told Pete on "The Nordy Pod" podcast, "Instead of working for Nordstrom, I made Nordstrom work for me. I use everything I can to make it a wonderful and beneficial [experience] for all. I don't sell clothes. I sell a feeling. It's about relationships." Although one of his regular customers is the famed singer-songwriter Ciara, Leggett said that in his eyes, "All my customers are high profile,"

With salespeople like Barnholdt and Leggett, Nordstrom continues to define and refine customer service.

"The best Nordstrom salespeople figure out how make it about them," said Pete. "It's their business. We're providing the infrastructure to make that business happen."

AGILITY IN A CRISIS

NORDSTROM IS NOT THE PERFECT COMPANY. The perfect company has yet to be invented. The Nordstroms will be the first to tell you that they have made—and will make—plenty of mistakes.

Jim, who was part of the third generation, once told *Footwear News*, "... we can't afford to boast. If we did, we might start to believe our own stories, get big heads and stop trying . . . Our success is simply a matter of service, selection, fair pricing, hard work. and plain luck."

Nordstrom people at all levels are especially reticent when it comes to talking about their reputation for customer service because, "We know that, at this moment, someone, somewhere, is getting bad service at Nordstrom," an executive once told me. "So we look good by comparison." There are times when a customer who received poor service would tell this Nordstrom executive, "If this had happened at Macy's, I would expect it. But this is *Nordstrom*."

In his memoir, *Leave It Better Than You Found It*, Bruce conceded that in the mid-1990s, he and John N., Jim, and Jack McMillan took their eye off the ball and didn't work as hard as they had in the 1970s and 1980s when Nordstrom was a retail juggernaut. By the end of the 1980s, the business had started to plateau. It wasn't dramatic, but the signs were there.

"Our business was doing well, and we were thinking, 'Gee, I can take one more day off a week and the business still does great,'" Bruce wrote. "We felt we had earned it, so we became interested in other things and took our focus off the business. We were all guilty of that; I am as critical of myself as I am of all of us. The fact is, the four of us weren't on the same page as much as we had always been in the past . . . We needed more energy because retail is energy."

Because the fourth generation was too young to take over leadership, the third generation tapped four of its most highly-regarded non-family executives to be co-presidents within an Office of the President. Bruce, John N., Jim and Jack became co-chairmen of the board. Within 18 months, it was obvious that structure was not working. Eventually, only one of those executives, John Whitacre, a respected, career-long Nordy, remained as president.

In the late 1990s, there was a decline in "same store sales" (stores opened at least one year, which is a key indicator in retailing), and stock shares were plummeting. The company was flailing," said Mike Koppel, who began his tenure as Chief Financial Officer in May 2001. "We were having a tough time generating profits. Growth slowed. Operating at a larger scale was challenging."

> "If someone has a bad experience at Nordstrom, it's personal. Not because we made it personal. It just is."
> –Jamie Nordstrom

Nordstrom was facing a crisis of confidence. The opinion of the media was summed up in a March 24, 1997 *Time* magazine double-page article that was headlined "Losing Its Luster," accompanied by a color photograph of a crushed Nordstrom gift box, wrapped in tattered ribbon. Ouch! This and similar stinging stories in *The New York Times*, *The Wall Street Journal*, and *Women's Wear Daily* questioned whether Nordstrom could turn things around.

But all was not lost. Nordstrom still maintained a loyal customer base. Loyalty is the capital of past trust. Nevertheless, loyalty is a double-edge sword. On one hand, loyalty enables businesses to gradually decline because customers don't abandon you overnight. On the other hand, loyalty gives businesses an opportunity to repair themselves for precisely the same reason: *customers don't abandon you overnight*.

> "We were afraid our reputation, status, and accomplishments were going out the window."

But Nordstrom was pushing the boundaries of that loyalty. A $40 million-advertising campaign in early 2000 called "Reinvent Yourself" focused less on merchandise and more on attitude and edge. For example, in an ad called "Reinvent Pajamas," the only item shown was a single strand of expensive pearls. Nordstrom was trying to attract a younger customer, but the ad campaign and store merchandise were out of the comfort zones of some longtime customers who felt alienated from the company they had known and loved. Executives were barraged with letters from angry customers who sent messages like this one: "You're telling me I have to reinvent myself? YOU go reinvent YOURself!"

This situation transcended business. It threatened the Nordstrom legacy—both family and business. Nordstrom had reached an existential crossroads.

"We thought we might lose this business," Bruce admitted. "Our reputation was still relatively untarnished, but our numbers told us that was not going to last very long. In those days, our family owned such a significant percentage of the stock that a corporate raider would have had a very difficult time attacking our company but might have been able to pull it off. We were afraid that our reputation, our status, our accomplishments were going to go out the window."

In the summer of 2000, the Nordstrom board was looking for new leadership. After undergoing a national search for candidates from outside the company, the board named Blake, then 39, to be president. Blake had been president of Nordstrom Rack Group and had been one of the co-presidents along with several of his cousins and his two brothers until that post was eliminated earlier in 2000. The board wisely decided that recruiting an executive who had not grown up in the Nordstrom culture was not a good option. A new executive would most likely rework the culture, cut overhead (mostly labor, Nordstrom's biggest expense) and perhaps even alter the company's liberal return policy. Then Nordstrom would no longer be *Nordstrom*.

Blake's father Bruce accepted the board's request for him to return as Chairman. A few days after Blake became President, his brother Pete was named President of Merchandising. Soon after, Erik, the youngest brother, was named Executive Vice President of Full-line Stores. He was later elevated to President of Nordstrom Full-line Stores. Like their grandfather, father, and cousins, Blake, Pete and Erik (and their cousin Jamie) began working in the store as young boys, sweeping floors and stocking merchandise before their fathers would ever let them near a customer. Life on the sales floor was where they all learned the rudiments of the business and, of course, customer service. This salesfloor-and-up approach promotes humility as well as a better understanding of how every aspect of the operation works.

"I have done nearly everything within this company that I am asking them to do (as have my cousins and my sons). I thoroughly understand the things about our business that aren't pleasant," said Bruce. "I don't know how you can run a business without firsthand experience. Because my sons have sold shoes (or as we call it, 'dogged' shoes), swept floors, and served as assistant managers, managers, and buyers, they come to their jobs with a knowledge of how things work and a respect for what it takes to succeed."

Pete noted, "I never felt like I got something that I didn't deserve. I was slugging it out just like everybody else. I don't know that I was any better than anyone else, but I certainly didn't think I was any worse."

Jamie, who began his career in 1986 in the stockroom and then sold shoes through high school and college, held positions in merchandise management, store management and buying. "You learn a lot about life in a stockroom," he noted. "You have to be a humble servant—literally. There's not a purer act of service than getting on your knees, measuring the customer's foot and tying their laces."

> ## "We learned what can happen
> ## if we get away from our culture."

Initially, Wall Street was unimpressed by the elevation of another family member to the top position. One so-called "expert" actually said: "I don't see this as much of a change. [Blake] talked about customer service and about listening to customers, the same platitudes we have heard before."

But it was those so-called "platitudes" that made Nordstrom Nordstrom.

If the selection of Blake received a lukewarm reaction from the outside, the response was much different from Nordstrom insiders who got the message that the family was ready to rejuvenate the company's unique culture.

"I would call the decision to promote Blake to president courageous but calculated," said Alfred E. Osborne, a Nordstrom director at that time, who has held the title of Professor and Faculty Director at the Price Center for Entrepreneurship & Innovation at UCLA's Anderson School of Management. "Nordstrom is like the swoosh of the Nike logo. When you see the Nordstrom logo, you know what it stands for. The culture is the secret sauce."

Mike Koppel, who rose to CFO at that time, recalled, "Analysts thought 'family' was almost a bad word. They didn't understand the importance of family at Nordstrom. All they saw was the family struggling to make Nordstrom a viable, growing, value-creating business. Culture beats strategy every time."

By going back to the basics—listening to employees and customers—Nordstrom turned things around. In 2004, the company recorded its fourth straight year of improved sales and profits. Nordstrom continued to be the most sought-after anchor store for mall developers because no other anchor had the power to draw such a broad cross-section of consumers. On August 19, 2004, a headline in the Wall Street Journal announced, "Nordstrom Regains Its Luster."

"Setbacks are sobering, but occasionally they are good for you," said Bruce. "In hindsight, going through that troubled period was a valuable experience for this company because it knocked right out the window any thought of our being a juggernaut. We learned what can happen if we get away from our culture."

TAKEAWAYS

- Agility requires courage and confidence

- Agility helps you respond more quickly to changes in the marketplace

- Cultivate long-term relationships

- Earn the right to ask for a favor

- Have the courage to ask for the sale

- Use technology to improve your customer's experiences

- Don't employ technology just for technology's sake

- Empower all employees to give customer service that goes the extra mile

- Stand for something (see "Tire Story")

- Don't become self-satisfied by your success

COMMUNICATION

*the act of transferring information from
one place, person or group to another*

C

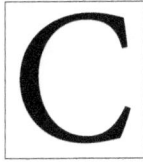

*When the trust account is high,
communication is easy, instant, and effective.*

— **Stephen R. Covey,** *The 7 Habits of Highly Effective People*

IN 2000, SOON AFTER BLAKE ASCENDED to the company presidency and his father Bruce returned to the chairmanship, their highest priority was reestablishing the lines of communication with employees. The Nordstroms knew it was imperative for them to connect in person to Nordies on the frontlines—the stores, distribution centers, and executive offices. Over a six-week period, Bruce and his sons Blake, Erik, and Pete fanned out across the country on a kind of "mea culpa" listening tour to reinvigorate a disheartened workforce.

Asking long-time top sellers and managers about how they viewed the state of the company, the Nordstroms received candid, unvarnished feedback. Blake would later recall, "They felt we didn't trust them anymore, that we weren't listening to them, and that we didn't value them as much."

Despite—or because of—the candid criticism, "I felt strangely invigorated," said Bruce. "I felt so good about the amount of input we got. We were heartened to find that our culture was not in shambles but was showing signs of weakening. People's spirits are much better when they're on a winning team. When the team loses, spirits go down. We were losing, and yet when I visited our stores, I saw our people smiling and giving good service."

The strength of the culture enabled Nordstrom to weather the challenges.

"When Blake became President, I asked him how he was going to bring the message to the frontlines," recalled Bob Schwartz, a former Nordstrom executive and long-time family friend. "Blake said, 'I'm going store-to-store and person-to-person, and drip, drip, drip our message over and over to one person, to groups, and to stores. I need to communicate to every employee our heritage and our stories.'"

One of the stories Blake liked to share was about his great-grandmother Hilda, the wife of founder John W. As Blake's dad Bruce wrote in his book *Leave It Better Than You Found It,* "Grandma was as sweet as grandmothers usually are, but to me, she was the tougher of the two, the one who wore the pants in the family. She was fiercely loyal to our company. When she found out that her milkman bought his shoes at Sears, she switched dairies."

It's not surprising that no one named Nordstrom is above doing a little housekeeping.

COMMUNICATE BY SETTING THE EXAMPLE

EVERETT, ELMER AND LLOYD SUBSCRIBED TO the "do-as-we-do" school of management, which has been emulated by their children and grandchildren. The Nordstrom philosophy is, "the willingness to do anything we'd ask someone else to do," a company executive told me. For example, unable to afford a janitor during the Depression, Everett, Elmer, and Lloyd arrived early every morning to vacuum the carpets and wash the outside of the windows.

"We felt that we should work harder than anyone else," wrote Elmer. "If we didn't, our lackadaisical attitude would spread to the next level, and the next level on down until everyone was taking it easy. We put in long hours, watched our overhead carefully, controlled our buying and markdowns, personally attended to every minor detail and worked closely on all matters. Our main concern was to pay for our store and achieve a solid footing . . . We got by."

So, it's not surprising that no one named Nordstrom is above doing a little housekeeping.

A woman who had worked at the downtown Seattle flagship Nordstrom store in the 1980s told me a story about the time Bruce walked through her women's apparel department. Spotting a can of soda pop that someone had left on a counter. Bruce picked up the can, deposited it in a wastebasket, and continued on his way. He didn't ask who was responsible for the can being on the counter. He didn't order an employee to throw it away. He never said a word to anyone. He just took care of it himself. The woman who shared this story went on to run several of her own successful businesses. And she never forgot the day she saw the chairman of the company demonstrate a behavioral standard that was both silent and eloquent. "If Bruce Nordstrom was not above doing a little housekeeping," she told me, "then neither is anyone else."

Although he uttered not a word, Bruce communicated a powerful message. That's what leaders do. When I related that story to Bruce, he was happy to hear it, but he had no personal recollection of what he did that day. Why should he? He was only doing his job.

"Today, if you walk around a store with one of our store managers or regional managers, you'll likely see them stopping to pick up trash or straighten a display, etc.," said retired Nordstrom executive Scott Meden.

ANSWER THE PHONE!

ANOTHER WAY NORDSTROM LEADERSHIP IS more accessible to the customer is by answering their own phone.

"My dad [Jim] always talked about the importance of answering your own phone. That was drilled into me at a very early age," said Jamie. "He told me about the time he was explaining to some European retailers how Nordstrom operates. My dad asked them if they answered their own phone. They said, 'Of course not. I have a secretary who does that for me.' My dad said to them, 'If you don't answer your own phone, then none of the rest of the stuff I told you is going to make any difference. You've got to support your people and your customers. If you don't demonstrate through words and actions that your customers and your frontline folks are the most important, then all the brilliant strategies aren't going to work.'"

Bruce estimated that over his career he took, "thousands of phone calls from customers who had one thing or another to say about how we were doing our business."

One day, he was working in his office when his phone rang, and he answered it: "Bruce Nordstrom."

After a moment of silence, the voice on the other end said, "Is this really Bruce Nordstrom?"

"Yes it is. How can I help you?"

After introducing himself, the caller explained that he was in Toronto, attending a seminar led by Tom Peters, author of *In Search of Excellence*. The seminar was on a break. Just before the break, Peters had told the audience he advocated that executives answer their own phones. But, he said, the only ones who do it are the Nordstroms. Before the start of the next session in the seminar, the happy caller told Peters and the rest of the audience that Bruce really did answer his phone. This pronouncement generated an enthusiastic round of applause. Peters later sent Bruce a thank-you note for validating what he had said, "and saving my bacon."

Decades later, Bruce's son Blake had a similar experience. An unhappy woman customer called Nordstrom's downtown Seattle flagship store and asked to speak to "someone in customer service." When her call was relayed, it went right to Blake's phone.

"Blake Nordstrom," he answered.

"Is this really Blake Nordstrom?"

"Yes, it is. How can I help you?"

"What are you doing answering the phone."

"I'm sitting at my desk, the phone rang, and I answered it," said Blake, who not only took care of the customer's service issue, but he also later took her to lunch, and established a friendship with her that lasted both their lifetimes.

"No comment" doesn't cut it

When I first started covering Nordstrom as a journalist in the 1980s, the company lacked a sophisticated communications and public relations operation befitting its size and increasingly high profile in the world beyond Seattle. At that time, management preferred the company name to appear in the media only when new stores were opening and when sales were up.

I recall the time in the late 1980s when the word was out in the industry that Nordstrom was going to open its first East Coast store in the Washington, D.C. market. An editor at *Women's Wear Daily* asked me to get a confirmation from Nordstrom and to find out the location and size of the store. Because he answered his own phone, I immediately was connected to Bruce (this was before he knew me personally). When I asked him to verify the story, Bruce basically said, "We're just out here in Seattle. We don't know what's happening on the other side of the country."

Quickly understanding that I was not going to get the answer I was looking for, I opted to play along with my future friend. "Let's pretend you were going to build a store in suburban Washington, D.C.," I said, "How big would you like it to be?" He laughed, and I laughed, but he still didn't give me what I was asking for. Years later, I told that story to Bruce, and we both enjoyed a good chuckle.

In 1988, the company opened its first East Coast store at the Tyson's Corner Shopping Center in Virginia.

"None of us in the third generation believed in public relations, which we thought was a waste of time and money, but we knew that our company had reached a size at which it was important," said Bruce. "We were never comfortable dealing with the media, and we avoided coverage if at all possible. We didn't want to tell our competitors what was selling, and we didn't want to show off. We try not to believe our own press clippings because too much praise is like a narcotic, and just as harmful."

Betsy Sanders, a now-retired company executive recalled attending an "unforgettable" managers' meeting in January

1972, four months after joining Nordstrom, which had recently gone public and had had a good year in a terrible economy.

"We were feeling pretty good about ourselves," said Sanders, who would go on to serve on the board of directors for several major corporations, including WalMart. "But the Nordstroms told us, 'We're afraid we're buying our own publicity instead of looking inward. There's only one goal that this company has to have in order for us to survive, much less thrive: We have to be the very best at customer service, by any standard. We know that you can't do it by yourselves, so we're going to help you in every way we can.' I was sitting there, listening to every word they said, and I took it for gospel. When I left the company 20 years later, our Number One goal was still the same: to be the very best at customer service."

In 1987, *Footwear News*, the industry's most important trade publication, named Bruce as Man of the Year. A modest man, Bruce was not interested in taking all the credit. In fact, he didn't want to accept the award, and declined to pose for the cover photo. *Footwear News* ran a sketch of Bruce instead. In 2005, when Nordstrom won the publication's Retailer of the Year award, Pete attended the ceremonies to accept the award on behalf of the company. He told the audience, "I'm here to give a mea culpa to the industry from my dad for not coming to New York to accept the Man of the Year award in 1987."

"We try not to believe our own press clippings because too much praise is like a narcotic, and just as harmful."

A HARSH LESSON

WITH THAT ARMS-LENGTH STANCE TOWARD MEDIA, it was not surprising that "crisis communication" was not a part of Nordstrom's corporate thinking.

As a result, in 1990, the Nordstroms were caught off-guard when they became embroiled in a highly publicized dispute with Local 1001 of the United Food and Commercial Workers Union (UFCW) that represented only the five Nordstrom stores in the Seattle-Tacoma metro area, representing 1,500 out of the company's 30,000 total employees.

In 1987, before new contract talks were initiated with the UFCW, many Seattle-area Nordstrom employees asked management to make union membership optional, i.e., to be an "open shop," which would represent a potential loss for Local 1001 of $3 million in annual dues ($7.6 million in today's dollars). The union fought back by alleging that Nordstrom forced managers to make employees work extra hours for "non-selling" activities such as writing thank-you notes, stocking inventory, attending meetings, and delivering merchandise to customers or to other stores—and not record those hours, which would have been a violation of Washington State wage-and-hour laws. Nordstrom denied the charges.

The UFCW did NOT dare call for a strike, which would NOT have been approved by the Seattle-area employees. In fact, the president of the local union was quoted in *The Wall Street Journal* that such a move would have been "suicidal," and that union support "has always been the weakest" at Nordstrom compared to employees at other major retailers. Instead, the union waged a negative publicity campaign against the company, filing a class-action lawsuit on behalf of 50,000 past and present employees in Washington, Oregon, California, Alaska,

81

Utah, and Virginia, charging a litany of "unfair" labor practices. The negative public relations culminated with a one-sided front-page article in February 20, 1990 edition of *The Wall Street Journal* that charged Nordstrom with taking advantage of and abusing their employees, who, the union claimed, were "suffering from ulcers, colitis, hives and hand tremors."

The article did quote Pat McCarthy, the highly successful men's suit salesman who originally worked with me on *The Nordstrom Way*, who said, "It's really a people job, which I love. Every year my sales have gotten progressively better."

McCarthy joined a group of employees operating under the name Nordstrom Employees Opposed to Union Representation (NEOUR), which held rallies outside Nordstrom stores in San Francisco, Southern California, and suburban Washington, D.C. in support of the company, and worked on decertifying Local 1001. (The National Labor Relations Board could have ordered a decertification election if more than 30 percent of employees petitioned for it, or if the company had evidence that more than 30 percent of members didn't want the union.)

Soon, the company brought in a seasoned Seattle public relations executive named David Marriott, "who calmed us down and advised us on how to proceed and how to get our side of the story out to the public," Bruce recalled.

> "The union did damage to us. On the other hand, it got our competitive juices flowing and became an incentive."

After *The Wall Street Journal* story, Nordstrom was approached by *60 Minutes*, the CBS-TV news magazine, to do a segment on the labor issue. Bruce called an emergency meeting of the family to discuss whether they should agree to be interviewed on camera. Faced with that critical decision, the Nordstroms relied on their decision-by-consensus approach, which requires flexibility and mutual respect.

"We were all sweating bullets about this whole thing," Bruce wrote in *Leave It Better Than You Found It.* "Jim, Jack, and I voted to do it, but John voted against it in the strongest of terms. We had always agreed that if one of us felt so strongly about something, we wouldn't do it. When we were finally about to give in to him, John said, 'If that's your decision, I support it.'"

Another example of the flexibility that makes Nordstrom Nordstrom.

Before the interview, *60 Minutes* correspondent Morley Safer, who was going to report the story, agreed to meet with the Nordstroms at Bruce's downtown Seattle condominium near Pike Place Market, "because we didn't want to be seen with him in public and he didn't want to be seen with us."

After some initial small talk, Bruce recalled, "We were sitting there, despairing, when suddenly our dog Stuffy, a funny little mutt, ran into the room and started scratching at Safer's leg, creating a cloud of hair and dandruff. 'Stuffy,' I said, 'get away from there!' Safer picked up Stuffy, put him in his lap, began to pet him, and said, 'I love dogs.' Stuffy saved the day."

Safer assured the Nordstroms that they would be treated fairly and would be given the opportunity for rebuttal. Confident in their position, the Nordstroms gave *60 Minutes* the run of the store. Producers could talk to anybody they wanted and could go into any department they wanted; even the stock rooms. (By comparison, the union had given *60 Minutes* a specific list of people they could talk to.).

When I tuned into *60 Minutes* the night of May 5, 1990 and saw that the Nordstrom segment was called "The Nordstrom

Boys" rather than "Retail Hell," I figured (correctly) they were home free.

At the time, Nordstrom was barely known outside the West Coast, so Safer explained to the national audience that, "Nordstrom is a phenomenon in the retail business. It actually offers service. Not service like it used to be, but service like it never was . . . Service is an act of faith at Nordstrom."

When Bruce told Safer on camera that he and his cousins, "were raised sitting on a shoe stool on our knees, sitting in front of a customer. That is both a literal and figurative posture. We understand that and we think our people understand that."

"A born servant," Safer said, with just a tinge of sarcasm.

"A born servant, if you will," Bruce quickly responded with a slight, tight smile. "Nothing wrong with that. We're proud of it."

Safer pushed the Nordstrom boys on the union grievances, and they pushed back in firm but gentlemanly fashion, with a light touch.

When asked about the UFCW's lawsuit against the company, one female salesperson said on camera, "We do not need outside influences breeding mediocrity and subjugating people," a line that took Safer aback. "*Breeding mediocrity and subjugating people?*," he asked in disbelief.

The producer of the *60 Minutes* segment, Marti Galovic Palmer, later told me, "A lot of what I was looking for in terms of hard complaints turned out to be from people who just wanted a job that didn't demand a whole lot. Basically, their attitude was 'It's a nice place to work, I like the job, but I don't want it to consume my life.' In the end, it was a little hard to get around that [stance] with a lot of the people that the union sent us." On the other hand, Galovic Palmer and her associates interviewed (on their own) many other salespeople who were "incredibly energetic and wanted it to consume their life."

The segment included an interview with a former employee who had worked in the men's department at a Nordstrom store in north Seattle. Alas, this young man had contracted HIV-AIDS, and had claimed that he was let go for that reason. The Nordstroms strongly denied the charge to Safer. Because he was physically weak and couldn't stand on the sales floor for a prolonged period of time, the salesman was offered the same pay, but for a non-sales job that did not require standing. Instead, he chose to quit.

The *60 Minutes* segment ended with that same young man being asked by Safer if he would come back to Nordstrom if given the opportunity. He replied that he would do so in a minute.

"That answer took all the wind out of the union's sails, and at that moment, we knew we had won," said Bruce. "We felt that we had successfully conveyed our message, and there was a better feeling among employees and customers."

Nordstrom did make a monetary settlement on the lawsuit, which was a small amount to get rid of the nuisance value. The union was never heard from again.

"The union did damage to us, no question about it," said Bruce. "On the other hand, it got our competitive juices flowing and became an incentive."

THE NORDY POD

TODAY, NORDSTROM HAS A SOPHISTICATED COMMUNICATIONS apparatus that is appropriate for its size and stature.

"Where we've evolved is to be more proactive vs. reactive in our external communications because people experience your brand across so many touchpoints," said Scott Meden, the

retired Chief Marketing Officer. "Also, we are more sophisticated in how we reach employees because we're too big and
spread out to rely solely on communicating in person. We use
video, email, and an intranet site to tell stories and communicate important information."

Proof of the company's modern approach is "The Nordy
Pod," Pete's biweekly free-form podcast—the first time a member of the family was front-and-center in a public-facing media
project. The podcast's target audience is both fashion industry
insiders and any consumer who has an interest in Nordstrom.
Pete's personal interests and connections guide the content
and creation, rather than tying it to the company's marketing
strategy. He has interviewed fashion industry luminaries such
as former Gap Inc. and J.Crew Group CEO Mickey Drexler,
and Steve Madden founder of the footwear company that bears
his name; actress and entrepreneur Jessica Alba,; rapper and
songwriter Macklemore, *Vogue* magazine editor-in-chief Anna
Wintour, as well as regular Nordstrom customers and rank-
and-file employees.

The podcast reflects Pete's curiosity: "Over the years, I've
found myself in some very interesting conversations with people
I greatly admire. These cumulative experiences have enriched
my life, and with 'The Nordy Pod', I'm excited to have the opportunity to share both professional and personal experiences."

Pete believes the podcast, "helps us articulate our values
and culture and our brand promise through stories and examples. It's another way to connect with customers and reveal the
authenticity and sincerity of what we're trying to do and why
we do it. We're a company of real people; a lot of humanity.
The podcast gives customers a window into what we're doing.
Transparency is increasingly important. Customers want to
be aligned with businesses that share their values. The more

transparent we are into how we are doing business and why we do what we do can only be a benefit."

At the end of each episode, Pete encourages listeners to communicate with the podcast via email or telephone: "We really want to hear about your experience with Nordstrom," whether "you have a story about how you received great service or even bad service."

"The Nordy Pod" is "a modern vehicle for expressing our culture and our values," said Erik. "I frequently reference the podcast and encourage our people to listen to it. It's really powerful to hear the company described by a vendor or a new intern or by people who have been here for 30 years. We believe in the importance of delivering a message—usually through a story—and weave in a lesson. Those stories reflect our culture and bind us together."

Internal Communication

Communication had to be more purposeful during the height of COVID, with stores shuttered and virtually every non-sales employee working from home.

With all the uncertainty, it was essential to be transparent about the challenges facing the company. In the midst of a crisis, teams need regular communication, honest information, and a tone of realistic optimism. There's no such thing as "too much communication." The Nordstrom strategy was to over communicate rather than under communicate.

As the Greek philosopher Aristotle wrote in the fourth century B.C.E., "All communication must lead to change."

"In a crisis, visibility is important," said Erik. "Our instinct for visibility was always to go out and visit stores. We couldn't do that, so we needed another form of communication. Our Executive Team met twice a day over Zoom in the first six months of the pandemic. A lot of decisions could be made only by the Executive Team. History was no guide. When do you declare the pandemic over? With our inverted pyramid, we want to push more decision-making upward. That doesn't happen organically."

It was up to Erik and Pete to get out messages that kept people connected to what the company was doing, and to sustain morale. After all, if no information and direction were dispensed from leadership, the void would have been filled with rumors, gossip, half-truths and misinterpretations. Nature abhors a vacuum.

For many weeks, every Friday they would send out a Zoom message to employees to keep them updated. Sometimes, the messages were given by Jamie (Chief Merchandising Officer) and Geevy Thomas, then President of Nordstrom Rack.

"This is the most difficult decision we've made in our company's long history because it impacts the people who matter most: you," said Erik on one of the Zoom calls. "Our company has survived wars, a depression, several recessions and natural disasters. The strength of our culture and the loyalty of our customers are what have sustained us through tough times. We can't predict what's next, but you have our commitment that we are here to support you and we will get through this. Everyone working during COVID is making it possible to weather this crisis and come out stronger."

"We believe in the importance of delivering a message—usually through a story—and weave in a lesson. Those stories reflect our culture and bind us together."

The Nordstrom brothers were initially wary of making themselves the center of attention. The family's trademark humility is legit.

"Broadcasting video messages out to 50,000 people was not something we went to naturally and quickly," Erik told me. "But intellectually, we understood that the more change there is, the more communication you have to have. We got a lot of positive feedback, which surprised us because we didn't think those videos were very impressive. But there was something to responding to a stressful situation with a message that, 'We're still here. It may be virtual, but we're still a team. We don't have all the answers, but we are going to get through this together.' That was a good lesson for us."

Before reopening brick-and-mortar stores, Nordstrom prepared shoppers for what to expect from the in-store experience by posting photos and videos of the upcoming changes through social media.

Some store layouts were reconfigured to create more space and promote one-way traffic flows. Customer capacity was limited; stores were cleaned more often; hours were reduced; and hand-sanitizer dispensers were scattered on every surface and liberally available. Store ambassadors were stationed at entrances to answer questions, to ensure customers maintained enough distance from each other, to manage the number of customers entering the store, and to give out disposable masks to customers who needed them. Signs conveyed checklists of, "What we're doing to keep you safe. Please maintain social distancing of at least six feet from others." After shopping, customers were checked out behind a plexiglass partition.

Recognition

Communication is the key to promoting employee engagement and development. Employees can be motivated, at least in part, by leadership's providing a vision and a clear mission statement. Nordstrom is constantly finding ways to praise and recognize its people because selling is tough, and customers can be tougher. Managers are responsible for providing those frontline people with support and encouragement.

Recognition, particularly in front of peers, is the most powerful incentive. That recognition, which must be sincere and honest, is usually the job of department managers. When individuals and departments are on target for reaching their sales goals, they are praised over the store intercom during the morning announcements before the store opens. Nordstrom rewards outstanding sales-per-hour and sales-per-month performance with cash prizes or trips, awards, and public praise.

During department meetings, managers will single out one or two people in front of their peers and recount how these particular employees gave great service to a customer or a co-worker. The manager might even put a rose in the employee's lapel for the day. Nordstrom communicates to those stellar employees that they are the kind of people they want others to emulate; the kind who live out the company values. They are reminded that Nordstrom wouldn't be as successful without them. It's powerful stuff.

A long-ago Nordstrom executive used to tell employees, "You're not good because you work at Nordstrom. You work at Nordstrom because you are good."

That message resonates to this day.

Nordstrom continues to set the bar higher for the people who want to be the very best, the people who hear about an award or an honor list or a contest and say, "I want to win that!"

At monthly Recognition Meetings, employees are honored for accomplishments such as departmental sales increases and promotional ideas that drive sales increases. These meetings are the company's biggest morale boosters because they double as pep rallies. Most important, they help to re-emphasize the culture. Although Nordstrom is a sales-focused organization, the company also recognizes acts of selfless customer service. Every month, store managers select their Customer Service All-Stars, who are evaluated on outstanding, consistent customer service and the level of support and teamwork they give their co-workers. This message is clear: If you're not a team player, you won't have a long career at Nordstrom.

The Customer Service All-Stars are not told in advance that they are being honored. But Nordstrom does secretly tell the All-Stars' families in advance and surreptitiously brings them to the Recognition Meeting. Imagine being honored in front of your peers, receiving a standing ovation, and then being happily surprised by the presence of your parents and/or spouse and children. It's a very emotional experience. The people who attend these meetings get so charged up, they take that energy back to their departments, and it spreads throughout the company.

> Communication is the key to promoting employee engagement and development.

The highest recognition at Nordstrom is the John W. Nordstrom Award, which goes to the manager who most exemplifies hard work, persistence, servant leadership, loyalty, honesty, ethics, competitive spirit, and an unwavering commitment to putting the customer first.

John W.'s great-grandsons, Pete, Erik, and Jamie, solicit nominations from regional managers, who in turn request them from store managers. They also seek out nominations from other company leaders and past winners from other parts of the company, such as merchandising and Human Resources.

Generating good sales numbers is one major criterion, but the winner must also be a selfless team player and committed to doing business The Nordstrom Way. The identity of the winner is known only to the handful of people who will keep it a surprise until it's announced at a Recognition Meeting in the region where the winner works.

Nordstrom likes to add a little drama to the proceedings, for maximum impact. While the regional manager conducts the meeting, all of a sudden the Nordstrom great-grandsons make their surprise entrance and take over the meeting. The employees erupt as if the Beatles had just shown up. Everybody knows that something special is about to happen. The Nordstroms playfully string out the crowd for a minute before they explain why they are visiting their store.

The winner is announced and dashes up to the front of the room. Just as in the Recognition Meeting awards segment, appearing from the wings are the winner's family members to share the moment. Tears and laughter. And the ultimate recognition.

New and past winners of the JWN Award attend an annual dinner in Seattle, hosted by the Nordstrom family. The company pays for travel and lodging for the winners and their guests, whether or not they're still working for the company.

Every year, top Nordstrom executives visit stores all over North America to give a "State of the Company" report. After two years of reporting via Zoom, in 2022 they resumed in-person meetings. Over a five-week period, executives hosted more than 260 gatherings in stores, fulfillment centers and corporate offices. The executives are transparent, sharing information on how the company is doing and where it's going. They are there to answer any and all questions. How many companies with 60,000 employees give their employees the opportunity to hear from company leaders in their own words?

How many companies believe in transparent communication? Does yours?

TAKEAWAYS

- Be transparent

- Give the news straight—good or bad.

- When disseminating your message be humble, authentic, respectful and strategic

- Communicate your values by example

- Internal communication—specific and unambiguous—is a hallmark of leadership

- Recognition and praise are essential to communication

TRANSFORMATION

a thorough or dramatic change in form or appearance

T

The only way you survive is to continuously transform into something else. Continuous transformation makes you an innovation company.

— **Ginni Rometty,** *retired chairman, president and CEO of IBM*

"OUR HISTORY OF SUCCESSFULLY NAVIGATING through transformation and tough times gives us confidence to go through the next transformation," said Erik, whose family-led company evolved from a tiny low-end shoe shop in 1901 Seattle (population 80,000) to today's national department store chain with the greatest high-end retail footprint in New York City (population 8.8 million) and online customers in 100 countries.

Every generation of Nordstrom leadership has at one time or another heard this lament from some long-time customers: "Nordstrom is not like it used to be." When Jamie hears that comment, he smiles and notes, "If we were like we used to be, we'd be gone."

Customers evolve and change over time, "not only in regard to the product, but how they like to be served," said Pete. "The best ingredient to success is to be reflective of what the customers are interested in." Generations of Nordstroms have diversified product offerings, broadened selections, partnered with new vendors (10 percent annual turnover), expanded geographically, added new store concepts, and invested heavily in digital technology.

For most of its history, Nordstrom exclusively hired from within, with virtually every buyer, manager, and executive starting their career on the sales floor and gradually working their way up. In more recent times, when Nordstrom opened stores in the U.S., the company would typically offer a mix of veteran employees from other Nordstrom stores, who carried the culture with them as well as new hires—many from rival retailers.

"Our hire-from-within philosophy evolved over time," noted Scott Meden, a 37-year employee who retired as Chief Marketing Officer. "While it made sense for a long time to fill almost all roles with internal candidates who had started in the store, that approach was no longer feasible if we wanted to secure the best talent in areas such as technology and digital marketing. Today, we have a healthy blend of internal hires (which ensures that path is still robust) and external hires that bring their unique skills and capabilities to Nordstrom."

Nordstrom leadership is keenly aware that the company must be current and fashionable in order to attract a younger customer and earn their loyalty, but not so cutting-edge that they leave behind older, loyal, legacy customers. (Average age of Nordstrom customers is around 46.) Consequently, Nordstrom walks a fine line and sometimes oversteps it, as proven by the customer pushback from the disastrous $40 million-advertising campaign ($89 million in today's dollars) "Reinvent Yourself" campaign of 2000, which focused less on merchandise and more on attitude and edge.

Metamorphosis on Main Street

I WROTE ABOUT ONE OF MY FAVORITE examples of transformation in my book *The Mom & Pop Store*: Galco's Old World Grocery in the Highland Park neighborhood of Los Angeles.

In the late 1990s, after almost one hundred years as a three-generational family-owned Italian grocery, the neighborhood was no longer significantly Italian in population. Galco's was facing its demise because ownership couldn't squeeze out the same profit margins that supermarkets enjoy on commodity grocery items such as soft drinks.

Owner John Nese told me that at his lowest point, "I was taking money out of my pocket and charging things on my credit card to keep the business going. We were right up against the wall." It was cheaper for Nese to buy Coca Cola or Pepsi Cola off the shelf at a rival supermarket than it was to get a case delivered from a wholesaler. With the fate of his family business on the line, Nese told his Coke and Pepsi sales representatives that he would no longer carry their products. The sales reps told Nese he was making a big mistake. Without realizing what they had done, "the Coke and Pepsi sales guys reminded me that *I* own my shelf space, and they don't, and I can sell anything I want."

Inspired by the popularity of beer from microbreweries, Nese started selling soda pop from boutique bottlers of soft drinks. He became an expert on the micro soda-pop industry and began searching for small bottlers from all over the United States, who shared his passion and vision. He decided that the soda pop he would carry must come only in glass bottles and must be made from only natural ingredients such as pure cane sugar (rather than corn syrup and essences), which are generally used in today's mass-produced sodas. He started out stocking twenty-five brands that had been famous in their regions of the country, such as Cheer Wine from North Carolina and Lemon Drop from Tennessee.

When Nese first displayed those items on his shelves, they were considered curiosities. "Customers asked me why I'm carrying old brands that don't sell anymore. When I got up to 250 brands, people started asking me where I was finding them. Now, we have five hundred brands" of every conceivable flavor, formula, product, and presentation, including cucumber and rose, which is pressed from rose petals.

The store is known online as Soda Pop Stop, with a Web site (www.sodapopstop.com) that has helped to spread the word all over the country.

Transformation is possible in any organization, regardless of size—once you know where you want to go.

> Moving into women's apparel, Nordstrom leadership was energized by the challenge of transformation. In that sense, they were once again a startup.

Transforming Through Opportunities

For many decades when the second generation of Everett, Elmer and Lloyd were calling the shots, Nordstrom operated dozens of leased shoe departments in department stores in the western United States and Hawaii. Under those arrangements, Nordstrom was responsible for the inventory, fixtures, managers and salespeople. The labels and shopping sacks had the name of the department store, and Nordstrom had to abide by the stores' rules. Nordstrom paid the stores a percentage of its volume, with a guarantee and a percentage override (commission).

"We had by far the biggest departments in these stores, and they represented pretty good cash-flow business for us," said Bruce. "They helped our financial picture and enabled us to be more flexible. On the other hand, we were invariably located in the third-rated department store in every town we were in. The leased operations didn't do much for our image and reputation. They weren't getting us where we wanted to be and were obviously not the future of our business. So when those stores started to have problems, we got out of them, thank goodness."

None of those stores exist today.

In the 1960s, Everett, Elmer, and Lloyd wanted to create opportunities for the third generation—Bruce, John N., Jim and Jack McMillan—so that they would stay with the company. Their options were either to open more shoe stores outside the Pacific Northwest (which they had outgrown) or diversify into another business.

Lloyd, the youngest brother who was only 53 years old at the time, wanted to make his own mark on the family business. The most stylish and sophisticated of the brothers, Lloyd was the prime instigator for the move into women's wear, which he felt would perfectly complement their traditional shoe business.

In 1963, Nordstrom acquired Best's Apparel, Inc., a fashionable downtown Seattle women's wear retailer, which had a second store in downtown Portland, Oregon. Best's carried primarily coats, suits and dresses aimed to a more mature demographic. (The brothers' decision-by-consensus conclusion to buy Best's is described in the chapter on Flexibility.)

Although Everett, Elmer, and Lloyd believed that if they could run a shoe store, they could run any retail business, their entry into apparel was initially met with skepticism by manufacturers who, "weren't very enthused to see us on buying trips,"

Elmer recalled. The company had a difficult time securing a lot of the hot lines that they wanted to buy. But the Nordstroms pressed on. The initial pushback from wholesalers, "reminded us of our early days in shoes. No one really believed that shoe store owners could be successful in apparel. No one except us. It was exciting because in many ways, *it was like starting over.*" [Emphasis mine.]

In other words, Nordstrom leadership was energized by the new challenge of transformation. In that sense, they were once again a startup.

Today, of course, virtually every apparel and footwear vendor would kill to have some real estate in a Nordstrom store.

Lloyd worked with the third generation of Bruce, John N., Jim and Jack to update the Best's image and merchandise in order to appeal to a younger group of fashion-conscious consumers: the ascending Baby Boom generation, at the impressionable time when their buying habits and loyalties were still being formed Catching the youth wave, Nordstrom added a juniors sportswear department. Men's and children's wear were added in 1966.

TRANSFORMING A SPECIAL SALE

BEST APPAREL HAD BEEN RUNNING AN Anniversary Sale every July since the mid-1940s. Owner Dorothy Cabot Best, a local tastemaker and influencer, stocked her store with finds from buying trips to New York. After acquiring Best's, Nordstrom continued the Anniversary Sale, which is not a promotion or clearance. Instead, it gives loyal, high-spending customers first crack at new fall merchandise priced at 25-40 percent off full price. After a publicized, designated date, the merchandise is sold at full price. The time frame gives customers greater incentive to buy before it's too late. Nordstrom has adapted the formula over the years, such as extending the length of the Sale and providing early access for holders of the Nordstrom credit card.

The Sale begins long before merchandise hits the racks. Devotees crunch numbers, devise game plans, and even book trips around the event. Today, the company utilizes the Nordstrom Analytical Platform—a real-time, event streaming–centric platform—that creates personalized digital catalogs with product recommendations for hundreds of thousands of its best customers. Other loyal cardholders gain access soon after, and eventually all shoppers gain access to the event.

The July Anniversary Sale has become an industry phenomenon, not only because of its popularity and revenue generator, but also because of its unique format that has yet to be successfully copied by competitors. In the 1990s, Macy's West Coast division tried, but they didn't stick to the idea of bringing in the best new product. The result was a hodgepodge of clearance items with a few new items.

For some people, Nordstrom's annual event is deadly serious. These are actual quotes from *The Seattle Times* archives:

"My father is dying but told me to go because it's only once a year."

"When I die, I'm going to be cremated and have my ashes scattered by Nordstrom. That way I'll always be close to my wife."

TRANSFORMING INTO A NATIONAL COMPANY

IN 1965, NORDSTROM OPENED ITS FIRST branch store at the Northgate Shopping Center near Seattle. Six years later, when the third generation took over, their strategy was centered around growth through store expansion in newly built shopping malls across the country. In 1964, there were 7,600 shopping centers in the U.S., and by 1990 there were 36,500 centers of all shapes, sizes and tenants. During the peak years of shopping center expansion, Nordstrom was the most sought-after anchor in the top centers because a commitment by Nordstrom was a crucial selling point to lenders. Nordstrom's emphasis on building full-line stores in primarily top level "A" malls allowed it to transform itself from a regional player to a national chain.

> Opening a store in South Coast Plaza
> was evidence the Nordstroms were flexible
> and agile and gutsy—just like a startup.

Throughout the 1970s, Nordstrom grew steadily. Although the company was known initially only in the Pacific Northwest, the third generation believed they could take Nordstrom national. The most logical next move would be to California; most likely San Francisco, the closest big city to Seattle

But instead of San Francisco, Nordstrom was invited to be a tenant in the upscale South Coast Plaza mall in Costa Mesa, California, in Orange County. Built and developed by Henry Segerstrom in 1967 on the site of what were once lima bean fields, South Coast Plaza had become one of the best shopping centers in the world.

"If Henry hadn't approached us, we would never have thought of going directly to Southern California, which seemed to us like another world," said Bruce. "To leapfrog all other possibilities, to go right to the number one shopping center—which was already anchored by Bullock's, May, Joseph Magnin, and Sears—was a major challenge. In addition to all that, Henry's terms were extremely tough, and building a store down there was going to be a major expense."

But the decision to open South Coast Plaza was evidence that the guys from Seattle were to be reckoned with; they were flexible and agile and gutsy—just like a startup should be.

"California was going to be Mecca," recalled Betsy Sanders, the Nordstrom executive who was put in charge of the move. "It was fraught with challenge, but it was exciting. There was no matrix, no plan, no instruction, which was also how Nordstrom worked. Except this was on a bigger scale than we normally did it. We invented this region as we went along."

The first California store was an instant success and became Nordstrom's highest-volume store at that time. Transformation through expansion.

INVENTORY MANAGEMENT: CENTRALIZED VS. DECENTRALIZED

FOR A GOOD PORTION OF ITS history—including the super growth era of the mid-Seventies to the mid-Nineties—Nordstrom was committed to decentralized buying and decision-making at the store level; not at headquarters. When Nordstrom was strictly a shoe retailer, store managers bought the inventory. (In the Foreword to this book, Steve Madden writes about his memories of those days.) When it added apparel, Nordstrom's individual, entrepreneurial salespeople were empowered to order out-of-stock items directly from the manufacturer. The company philosophy at that time was that a buyer had to be on the floor to learn what items the customer was asking for that Nordstrom didn't have. Management's quick response to that immediate feedback helped to solidify customers' loyalty.

"My cousin Jim and I were the last holdouts as far as thinking that we never wanted to centralize this business," said Bruce. "I had to be sold on technology because I felt that the decisions had to be made by the people who were actually on the firing line. In the old days, at the end of every day the manager would have each salesman turn in the list of the things he had sold, then compile them in a book. It was all done by hand."

In 1996, just before he passed away far too soon at age 56, Jim told me a story he heard from his grandfather John W., about his differences with his partner and co-founder Carl Wallin:

> One day, Wallin was out to lunch with a vendor and my grandfather was in the store by himself. A big Swede walked in and wanted a pair of size 12 shoes. We didn't have any. We only carried up to size 11, so he lost the sale. He called the vendor of that shoe and ordered a pair of brown and black dress shoes in size 12. When the shoes came in, Wallin told my grandfather, "We can't make any money carrying size 12 shoes."
>
> That really ate at my grandfather because he always felt that if someone comes into the store and asks for something it's our job to get it for them. He didn't know any other way to run a business.
>
> As we grow, always remember that the person on the floor makes the call on what we should carry because they are the one who's having the experience with the customer. If we listen to the person on the floor, then we will have good inventories. My grandfather's sons believed that; so have Bruce, John, Jack and me, and I hope the next generation continues to believe in that.

Nordstrom could not endure without a clear understanding of the differences between legacy practices and values.

LEGACY PRACTICES VERSUS LEGACY VALUES

THE DECENTRALIZED APPROACH WORKED FOR MANY years until the company grew too big, and inventory flow and supply chain technology became more important to profit margin.

"Technology gave us visibility that was impossible to have at scale, said retired Chief Marketing Officer Scott Meden, a 37-year Nordy who began his career selling shoes. "Knowing what we sold and owned, and knowing the sell-through by style, color, size, location was a powerful shift. Even when we had a buyer in every store, you couldn't see and understand what was happening with inventory at that level of detail."

Decentralization was not a *value*; it was a *practice*. The value lies in (1) understanding what the customer wants and (2) creating a compelling journey of discovery by exposing customers to brands and trends they didn't know they wanted. For transformative companies, all legacy practices must be constantly reexamined and reevaluated, but values must never change.

"The business is completely different from when Erik and I started," noted Pete. "There's no way the company would have made it if we didn't have a clear understanding of the differences between legacy practices and values. Once we got our head around that, we were open to other ideas. If we were tied to legacy practices, we would have flamed out."

Continually talking about values vs. practices helps challenge Nordstrom to change.

"We don't change the value; we change the practice," said Erik. "We want to center people on the cultural aspects of the company that they really like, which gives them the confidence to change. In the old days, decentralized buying served us well because we didn't have the merchandise information systems. Today, we have the systems to do that, to get customers what they want when they want it."

NORDSTROM 1.0 AND NORDSTROM 2.0

THROUGHOUT MOST OF ITS HISTORY, "Nordstrom 1.0" was a conventional brick-and-mortar retailer, serving one customer at a time through a salesperson who connected with the customer. Nordstrom Rack was established in 1975, when the Nordstrom family opened a clearance section in the basement of the downtown Seattle store. Eventually, they expanded the concept with Nordstrom Rack clearance stores that sell 90 percent of the top brands sold at Nordstrom's full-line stores, as well as additional specially-purchased product at 30-to-70-percent discounts.

By 1989, the Rack concept was so successful that it became a separate division. Racks generally range from 30,000 to 50,000 square feet, compared to full-line, full-price stores that range in size from 120,000 to 380,000 square feet. Because Racks have a positive impact on sales at nearby full-line stores, the company strategically locates them as close as possible to full-line Nordstrom stores. A 42,500-square-foot Rack is located right across the street from the downtown Seattle flagship store.

"The Rack was Blake's legacy," said retired Nordstrom Rack president Geevy Thomas, . "He was the champion and driving force of Rack. It's the biggest source of new customers as well as the biggest source of talent acquisition and development. The stores have the highest sales-per-square-feet in the off-price business."

"Nordstrom 2.0," which arose in the late 1990s with the arrival of e-commerce, comprised a set of digital customer touchpoints.

"The biggest, most transformative and revolutionary thing that's happened in our generation is the digital business," said Pete. "It was not a conscious decision to take a big gamble. It happened organically."

Nordstrom.com launched in 1998—three years after the launch of Amazon.com, its neighbor in Seattle. By that time, Nordstrom was led by a younger generation that understood the potential of online shopping. Nordstrom has long invested in digital and physical resources to keep pace with customers' ever-more-demanding expectations. COVID-19 accelerated the importance of these capabilities in serving customers.

Nordstrom 3.0: Closer to You

"Nordstrom 3.0" is centered around what was originally a marketing idea, created in 2021, called "Closer to You," which was a way to describe the overall strategy—closer in both the physical and digital worlds because the consumer journey is no longer linear. Customers demand service that is integrated across all channels.

"Closer to You" initially sounded like an ironic message in the middle of a pandemic where people were told to observe "social distancing." Nevertheless, to Nordstrom management it felt right because, "Closer to You is about having a relationship," said Erik. "We still need to make connections with customers. We are not a transactional retailer."

The physical store is not dead; it's digitized.

Nordstrom 3.0 provides a greater assortment of services, conveniences and options that result in deeper engagement by shoppers.

This current approach personalizes the company's digital platform (Nordstrom.com and NordstromRack.com, which launched in 2014; the Nordstrom app and social media) while utilizing its brick-and-mortar assets including full-line stores, Rack clearance stores in shopping malls and selected downtowns, and a new store concept called Nordstrom Local, which the company unveiled in 2018 with two units in the Los Angeles area. (The cover of this book features a Local in Newport Beach, California.)

In the 2020s, faced with an increasingly competitive off-price retail sector, Rack's performance hit a slump. The company brought in new leadership and created a new brand identity and logo to transform Rack's perception among consumers. In the logo, the word "Rack" is dominant, while the word "Nordstrom," shown above "Rack" is in smaller letters.

Nordstrom Locals are approximately 3,000-square-foot neighborhood stores that contain no merchandise. These are service hubs for online order pickup and returns, clothing donations, gift-wrapping, express alterations (fun fact: Nordstrom is the biggest employer of tailors in the U.S), and free fashion guidance, advice and tips from professional stylists.

Local is designed to be an easy, fast, zero-pressure, and frictionless customer-centric experience that is ideal for certain urban environments because they are about convenience.

Immediately embraced by customers in Southern California, two more Locals were added in the L.A. area, and later two more in Manhattan—one on the Upper East Side and one in Greenwich Village, which is toward the Lower West Side of the island.

Because return rates are higher for online purchases, Nordstrom encourages customers to initially search for and discover products online before visiting a Nordstrom store to touch and try on items before deciding to make a purchase.

"We want to be there when, where and how the customer wants to shop our network including full-price and off-price stores, sites and apps that are increasingly connected," said Scott Meden, the retired Nordstrom executive.

This system—Buy Online, Pickup In-Store (BOPIS)—represents shopping on the customer's terms and is one of the fastest-growing parts of the company's business. COVID accelerated the popularity of the strategy. Other primarily brick-and-mortar retailers have also been successful with BOPIS.

Nordstrom considers itself "Channel Agnostic. The company doesn't believe customers think in terms of shopping by channels, whether brick-and-mortar store or website or app. "We don't care where they shop, We don't have online customers or store customers; it's one customer," said Erik. Customers go back and forth seamlessly between channels, which is why Nordstrom has never tried to dictate to customers which channel to shop. Essentially all of the stores serve as warehouses for the online business.

The physical store is not dead; it's digitized. Nordstrom has long believed we live in an omnichannel retail marketplace where brick-and-mortar stores are an essential part of the equation. Retail must encompass both the personalization and sensory experience of the physical store and the personalization and convenience of digital. The most successful retailers seamlessly blend both. As John Zissimos, a digital marketing expert, has said, "We are now in the fourth industrial revolution, a blurring of the physical and digital worlds—with customers at its center." Nordstrom has always put the customers at the center. Today, they have more ways to do just that.

> Nordstrom has evolved from being a curator of products to being a curator of service and experience, supported by product.

Nordstrom continues to increase the number of people who shop via more than one channel, because those customers spend an astonishing 12 times more than a customer shopping a single channel. "The more we engage with customers, the better everything becomes. It leads to increased spend and loyalty," said Erik.

Consider these numbers:

- More than 50 percent of customers who shop in a brick-and-mortar Nordstrom store will have started their shopping journey at Nordstrom.com

- One-third of all new customers come via Nordstrom.com

- More than 25 percent of Nordstrom.com orders are fulfilled in the stores

- Customers who take advantage of Nordstrom's in-store pickup spend 3.5 times more than customers who don't

- Customers who use services such as alterations and personal styling spend more than customers who don't by a factor of 5 to 7 times

- Customers that interact or engage in Nordstrom Local spend 2.5 times more than the average customer

As part of its digital-first "Closer To You" strategy, Nordstrom in 2022 launched the Nordstrom Media Network, which helps the company stay closer to its customers by partnering with key brands and introducing those brands to customers. The Media Network affords these brand partners a platform for connecting directly with 32 million Nordstrom customers (representing nearly 2 billion annual visits) in the form of advertising opportunities, direct-response marketing, personalized recommendations, and sales. The participating brand partners acquire customer data that helps them (and Nordstrom) customize how they advertise and sell.

"We are really good at exposing customers to new brands and introducing those new brands to customers. And customers come to us less so for price promotions, and [more so] for newness," Erik told a Morgan Stanley Global Consumer and Retail Conference at the end of 2022. "In particular, a sweet spot for us is not necessarily launching new brands, but brands that are in an early stage and hitting their growth stride. That's where we can really help them scale."

Nordstrom will continue to transform itself through its investments in technology in supply chain and merchandising, including additional enhancements to its buy-online-pick-up-in-store (BOPIS) and curbside pickup programs, which are popular with customers and profitable for the company.

The goal is for the supply chain to be personalized for each customer by leveraging physical space and technology like robotics and automation. It means not only having the right product at the right time—a time-honored Nordstrom approach—but also being closer to customers' homes and communities by providing in-store order pick-up, returns, and services in the customer's preferred location, be it home, office or their closest Nordstrom store.

When most people visit a store to exchange an item for the right size, they usually buy more stuff.

"Non-verbal" Communication

NORDSTROM COMMUNICATES BY PROVIDING CUSTOMERS with speed and convenience, which convey the message, "You asked us, and we heard you."

The company brings in customers and employees to its Convenience Center lab to test and provide feedback on initiatives for enhancing personal communication between customers and salespeople, and to find ways to support the retail needs of time-starved and self-directed shoppers at any touchpoint of their shopping journey. Nordstrom values meaningful "engagement" more than an individual sale in any particular visit.

When a customer visits a store to pick up an online order or to make a return, they may not be in a buying mode. Nevertheless, Nordstrom believes that if it handles those transactions as rapidly as possible, the customer will return to shop. Although there was some initial pushback from the stores about dealing with the returns and taking them off their profit & loss statements, stores adapted because Nordstrom leadership and staff learned that when most people visit a store to exchange an item for the right size, chances are they will buy more stuff.

Taking back returns also must have a customer service element. Items sold through Nordstrom.com include a pre-paid, self-addressed FedEx envelope.

As an added feature, Nordstrom Local accepts merchandise returns from Macy's and Kohl's, regardless of whether Nordstrom carries the same item.

COMMUNICATING LOYALTY

THE NORDY CLUB, NORDSTROM'S LOYALTY PROGRAM, is a key part of the brand. Nordy Club members can earn rewards, gain early access to new merchandise, and take advantage of exclusive personalized services such as house calls from stylists. "Nordstrom Notes" can be redeemed toward purchases of qualifying items in stores or online.

Through their own digital profile, customers can customize their style profiles, manage their brand preferences, and keep track of their accumulated earned points, which shows how much they need to spend to reach the next level of loyalty. Each tier of the loyalty program grants access to more perks.

Members of the loyalty program tend to make purchases more often than those who are not. The retailer's more than 10 million active members spend 4X more and shop 3X as often than non-member customers.

As of this writing, a slight majority of Nordstrom's business comes through the loyalty program, which is another way to be in communication with customers that deepens the relationship.

Reflecting on shaping the loyalty program, Nordstrom's then-Chief Technology Officer Edmond Mesrobian told *Women's Wear Daily* in 2022, "The challenge is the world is moving from being transactional to one of engagement." It's not just about earning points for purchase, he said. "Loyalty is a vehicle for experience—invitations to a party, a fashion show, early access to fashion—not just transactions. That's on our journey toward engagement as our North Star."

> Nordstrom transforms its offerings by creating new partnerships and cooperative agreements with vendors.

PARTNERSHIPS

OVER ITS LONG HISTORY, NORDSTROM has transformed itself through acquisitions, investments and strategic alliances, learning from them and making them a part of their overall offerings.

From 2000 to 2007, the company owned Façonnable, an upscale European collection apparel for men and women, which some people compare to the preppy Ralph Lauren Polo line. In 2005, they purchased a majority interest in Jeffrey, two luxury fashion boutiques in Atlanta and New York City. In addition, Nordstrom hired founder and namesake Jeffrey Kalinsky to be director of designer apparel merchandising.

In 2011, Nordstrom acquired Los Angeles-based HauteLook, a member-only shopping website that offered flash-sales and limited-time sale events for apparel, jewelry and accessories at discounts of 50 to 75 percent. In 2021, Nordstrom phased out HauteLook and moved its flash sales business to NordstromRack.com. In 2012, Nordstrom became the only major U.S. retailer to sell a broad assortment from the renowned British fashion brands Topshop and Topman. In 2014, the company acquired Trunk Club, a personalized online clothing service with seven stores. In 2021, Trunk Club was folded into Nordstrom's offerings and the stores (known as "clubhouses") were closed. This category also was challenging for Stitch Fit, Trunk Club's chief competitor, which by the end of 2022 reported losses for three years in a row, cut its workforce by 20 percent, and replaced its Chief Executive Officer.

Nordstrom continues to transform its offerings by creating partnerships and cooperative agreements with its vendors. For example, taking a page from Amazon.com's marketplace approach, Nordstrom works jointly with direct-to-consumer brands that sell products via their own websites and through brick-and-mortar retailers.

Nordstrom believes the best brands know their consumers best, which means those brands are better able to fulfill the desires of their consumers. Under Nordstrom's "concessions model," selected wholesalers can manage their brand imaging, presentation, in-store shop design, and website look, as well as sales staff, pricing, shipping and ownership, control, and flow of its inventory. Typically, the brand keeps most of the sale while the host (Nordstrom) takes a commission. This idea is not new. Department stores have taken the same approach for a century. As previously discussed, Nordstrom used to be on the other side of that relationship in the 1940s and 1950s when the company ran leased shoe departments in several department stores in the Western U.S.

The concession model benefits Nordstrom in two ways: (1) Because the brand is essentially operating their own shop-in-shop, Nordstrom cedes ownership of the inventory and eliminates the risk of buying the wrong merchandise; and (2) Because the brands are better able to serve and satisfy their own customers, Nordstrom will make a greater profit.

NORDSTROM HAS EVOLVED FROM BEING A curator of products to being a curator of service and experience, supported by product. Under the traditional model, retailers like Nordstrom bought merchandise at wholesale from brands and then sold the merchandise to customers who visited their stores. Today, there are many different ways for customers to buy merchandise: stores and online, consignment, and pre-owned.

"We are not in 100-percent wholesale relationships," said Erik. "To get the selection that customers want, given the times we are in, we have drop-shipping from the vendor; we have consignment where we don't own the inventory."

Recognizing that many consumers are eschewing ownership of product, Nordstrom experimented in a partnership with Rent The Runway, an e-commerce platform that allows users to rent, subscribe to, or buy designer apparel and accessories. Nordstrom incorporated Rent The Runway inventory into its platform and offered an option for returning the rented items to self-service drop box kiosks at selected Nordstrom full-line and Local stores.

Nordstrom has also experimented with the resale luxury business in stores with a department called "See You Tomorrow," which included women's apparel and shoes; handbags; men's apparel, accessories and shoes; kids wear; and a limited selection of jewelry and watches. Unlike other retailers, Nordstrom sourced from its own inventory. These are garments that have been returned by customers (Nordstrom has a liberal return policy) and then cleaned and (if necessary) repaired.

"We are connecting our customers to that product offering," said Erik. "It's not easy building a system to support that. We used to pooh-pooh any model where we didn't own the inventory ourselves. We like controlling the customer ask. We think having flexibility in our inventory ownership models is essential."

"I don't think we are great at making an unknown brand known," conceded Pete. "But we are good at making a known brand bigger and better."

To boost store traffic and drive sales. the company also is working with small direct-to-consumer brands with negligible brick-and-mortar presence. These brands cover a wide variety of product categories such as men's and women's apparel; luxury plus-size apparel for women; licensed sport merchandise; aromatic candles; bed mattresses; cosmetics; and home-gym equipment. Nordstrom gives these partners creative flexibility and shares data with them. The target goal is for strategic brands to comprise about 50 percent of full-price sales.

Nordstrom had never been a significant factor in the home furnishings business, which has traditionally been the bailiwick of specialty stores and e-commerce websites as well as traditional large department stores such as Macy's and Target. But with online becoming a bigger part of its business, the company saw an opportunity to make inroads into the home category with a wider product selection. "We are working with new brands that have the flexibility to do what we can to partner together," said Jamie. "The perfect scenario for us is to have a well-known, highly-sought-after brand that you can't find in a lot of places." For the spacious Manhattan store, the approach was to find cool, unique items that add a fun, serendipitous sense of discovery to the in-store retail experience.

THE LOSS OF BLAKE

IN LOOKING BACK ON THE CHANGES and challenges of Nordstrom's 120-plus-year history, the sudden, unexpected passing in January 2019 of Blake at age 58 was especially profound on both a personal and business level. It was transformative.

Personally, my earliest memory of Blake goes back to 1993. While researching *The Nordstrom Way*, I attended my first employee orientation meeting. After the twenty or so new "Nordies" viewed a twelve-minute video on the history of the company entitled "The Nordstrom Story," a tall, smiling, blond-haired, 33-year-old, walked to the front of the room to address the group.

"I like to come to these meetings and meet our new people," he said warmly. "My name is Blake and I'm really excited to have you here." At the time, Blake was vice-president and general manager of the Washington state and Alaska group of stores, and later president of Nordstrom Rack Group. "The first thing we tell new employees is that there's nothing new in customer service," Blake continued. "We are fond of saying that the best training you can have is your parents. Did they teach you to be nice, and smile, and work hard?"

As I watched him address the new employees, one thought popped into my head: "That's the future leader of Nordstrom."

And that's eventually what happened. In the summer of 2000, the Nordstrom board named Blake, then 39, to be president. He had been one of the six co-presidents of his generation.

Blake was the embodiment of the Nordstrom service culture; he walked the talk. Here's one of my favorite Blake stories: In 2006, he appeared on the Public Broadcasting Service television program "CEO Exchange" with Jim Donald who at the time was CEO of Starbucks, and a Seattle neighbor of Blake's. On the morning of a day the two executives were scheduled to meet for lunch, Donald asked Blake if he wouldn't mind first stopping off at Nordstrom's men's apparel department to bring two pairs of slacks that had been altered. Blake agreed, but by the time he was ready to meet Donald for lunch, he had forgotten to pick up the slacks. Donald had forgotten he had made the request.

"That evening at 9 o'clock, there's a knock at my door," Donald told the audience. "I opened the door and there was Blake carrying those two pairs of pants and apologizing for forgetting them at lunch. I said, 'Man, that's what I call service.'"

Emulating the second and third generations' collaborative, decision-by-consensus approach, Blake, Erik, and Pete made an effective team. Before they were colleagues, they were close-knit brothers. Blake was born October 4, 1960, Pete on February 14, 1962 and Erik on October 24, 1963. And they genuinely liked and respected each other. Bruce gave most of the credit to the boys' mother, Fran, who was an at-home mom and primary caregiver. The brothers became even closer when Fran passed away from cancer in 1984.

"We worked so hard to be a good team of three," said Pete. "There was a dynamic. The three of us had different roles and we each worked hard to pull our weight. None of us wanted to be the loser of the group. [The members of the previous generations had that same competitive spirit.] That affects everything. Blake would always take the toughest job. If bad news had to be announced, he was the one who did it. That was the older brother part of him."

One of the company's most momentous decisions was to build the 350,000-square feet store in mid-town Manhattan.

The building's most striking feature and statement is a double parabolic S-curve-shaped glass façade that captures the sunlight in ways flat glass can't. Rising five stories high and 150 feet across, the glass required special engineering and manufacturing, because only three ovens in the world were large enough to curve glass of this scale. It was engineered in Italy, manufactured in Germany, bent in Spain, and framed in the United States. The facade was Nordstrom's opportunity to connect to the city. The whole store becomes a window to the street.

Dawn Clark, then Senior Vice President of Store Design, Architecture and Construction, told me she once was asked to make a last-minute presentation on the glass façade for the approval of the board of the directors. With no formal presentation prepared, Dawn grabbed a full-scale printout of the waves, took it into the boardroom and rolled it out in the long corridor outside the executive offices. She asked Blake what he thought of the idea of presenting it there. Blake loved it. He went into the boardroom and invited everyone to come out into the hall to see the printout. The glass waves were enthusiastically approved by the board.

Blake constantly visited Nordstrom stores around North America and interacted with employees (as his brothers and Jamie still do.)

"Blake could never have been on the television program 'Undercover Boss' [in which a chief executive wears a disguise while performing low-level tasks in their company] because everyone would have recognized him," joked Geevy Thomas, a retired, long-time Nordstrom executive.

"Blake was one of the greatest communicators I ever knew," said retired CFO Mike Koppel. "When I traveled with him, I felt like I was traveling with Bono from U2. He attracted people. He remembered them, knew their names, told stories."

On the day that Blake passed away, I kept reading all the tributes and memories that people shared on the "Nordstrom Friends" Facebook page. This one from Nordstrom salesperson Romey Rancharan is one of my favorites. When Blake stopped by a women's wear department at the Costa Mesa, California Nordstrom store, Romey didn't know who he was.

> *He was wearing a suit and I thought he was from Corporate. He looked around and said, "What can I do for you?" I replied, "You can help me tear these boxes open if you want." He agreed to it and there we were ripping boxes open. At the end I thanked him and thought, what a nice guy. My co-worker said, "Do you know who that is?" I said, "No, but he was sweet and cute." She said, "That was Blake Nordstrom. He shouldn't be ripping boxes open." I said, "He wanted to." She was like, "Good for him." Thank you Mr. Nordstrom.*

After Blake's death, Erik became Chief Executive Officer and Pete was named President and Chief Brand Officer. Blake left a void as a business colleague and as a brother.

"I miss him more as a brother," said Pete. "He was a great older brother. People who admired and loved Blake wanted Erik and I to do what he did; to be him. There are things about him that I can't replicate. It's not a big burden for me."

As brothers, teammates and leaders of the company, "We didn't care who got credit," said Erik. Although Blake had a conservative business aura about him, "It may surprise some people to know that Blake liked big change. He liked when times were tough. He got a lot of energy and clarity. I could worry about something else because Blake was that rock. He'd say, 'Things are going to be okay.' To suddenly not have that . . ."

(In the Foreword, Steve Madden fondly recalls his memories of Blake.)

In two sections of the Manhattan store are Blake's shoe prints cast in bronze. The footprints in the shoe department are a tribute to his years of selling shoes and watching the floor. Blake, like the other Nordstroms, was at heart a merchant. When it came down to his leadership and teamwork, Blake's impact was transformative.

Takeaways

- Every organization must be in a perpetual state of transformation

- Always search for new opportunities

- Be open to new ideas

- Evolve and appeal to customers across a broad age spectrum

- Understand the differences been legacy values and legal practices

- Make transactions easier to customers so they give you more business

- Give customers reasons to be loyal to you

- Give customers options for ways of doing business with you

SOCIAL RESPONSIBILITY

*an ethical framework in which individuals and organizations
work and cooperate for the benefit of the community*

S

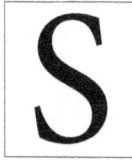

Leave it better than you found it.

— **Bruce Nordstrom**

BEFORE THERE WAS MICHAEL JORDAN, THE best player in the history of the Chicago Bulls was Bob "Butterbean" Love. The 6' 8" forward grew up in rural Louisiana and played at Southern University a public historically black land-grant university in Baton Rouge. He competed for 11 seasons in the National Basketball Association from 1966 to 1977, most of them with the Bulls, and was the team's leading scorer for seven straight years. Pre-Jordan, Love held all of the Bulls' scoring records and was a three-time NBA All-Star.

Unfortunately, Love had a severe stutter, which kept him from being able to endorse products or to be interviewed by the media. In the years in which he competed, player salaries were a tiny fraction of what they are today. Toward the end of his career, he was traded to the Seattle SuperSonics, where he played for one season before a bad back forced him to retire in 1977 at the age of 35. Love went through crushing adversity—losing his money, his wife, and some of his self-respect. After a challenging job search in Seattle, Love, who had a degree in food and nutrition, was hired to bus tables and wash dishes in the restaurant in the Nordstrom flagship store in downtown Seattle, where he was paid $4.45 an hour.

It was hard to miss this 6' 8" Black man cleaning tables. Love could hear the whispers: "Hey, that's Bob Love. He used to be a great basketball player. What a shame."

Love was undeterred. "I never played the victim. It didn't hold me back. I just tried harder. I was going to do the best job I can do. The Nordstroms gave me an opportunity and I was not going to blow that opportunity."

After working for year and a half at Nordstrom, Love was taken aside by co-chairman John N. of the third generation, who told him, "We think you could have a future with our company, and we'd like to help you get your life together. But first you'll have to do something about your speech," Love wrote in his book *The Bob Love Story*.

"It was the opportunity I'd been waiting for," wrote Love. "It seemed as though the weight of the world had suddenly been lifted from my shoulders. It had been years since anyone had shown that kind of personal interest in me." For the first time since I was a child and my grandmother had taken care of me, I felt that someone was concerned about me as an individual. It didn't have anything to do with basketball or being an athlete, it was about me as a human being."

Love accepted the Nordstroms' offer of help. Eventually, for the first time in his life, Love could speak without being stopped by his stutter. He ultimately rose up through the ranks to become a diversity affairs manager for Nordstrom. Eventually, he was hired by the Chicago Bulls to become their Director of Community Affairs, speaking to young people in schools all over the Chicago area. Even more impressive is the fact that, Bob Love became a highly sought-after inspirational and motivational speaker.

"I'm still speaking to kids," he told Pete on The Nordy Pod podcast. "I'm telling my story and the Nordstrom story to everybody. Nordstrom is a big part of my life. I love Nordstrom."

And how does the greatest player in Bulls history feel about the player who once held all the Bulls' scoring records? Well, the introduction to "The Bob Love Story" was written by none other than Michael Jordan.

The World Business Council for Sustainable Development defines Corporate Social Responsibility as, "the continuing commitment by business to behave ethically and contribute to economic development while improving the quality of life of the workforce and their families as well as the local community and society at large."

The Bob Love story is the quintessential example of that commitment.

> You can't create a place where you treat customers well if you don't first treat each other well.

CORPORATE SOCIAL RESPONSIBILITY

"BUSINESSES MUST RECONNECT COMPANY SUCCESS with social progress," wrote Michael E. Porter, the Harvard Business School professor and author of *On Competition*. "Shared value is not social responsibility, philanthropy, or even sustainability, but a new way to achieve economic success. It is not on the margin of what companies do but at the center."

Nordstrom's Corporate Social Responsibility initiatives focus on four areas: (1) Making Nordstrom a better place to work; (2) Giving back to the communities it serves; (3) Protecting the environment; (4) Protecting Human rights, especially in countries where Nordstrom's private label products are made.

These initiatives, "reflect the kind of company that the right people want to be associated with," said Erik. "Our efforts in this area add clarity to our mission. We're sensitive about our reputation as an employer. You can't create a place where you treat customers well if you don't first treat each other well. We have to be a great place to work."

This company was founded by an immigrant, John W., who came to America to build a better life. Today, many of Nordstrom's top grossing salespeople were born in other countries, and like John W., they embrace the opportunity to live the American Dream.

Ever since the 1930s, Nordstrom had set the wage standard for Seattle retail workers. In Nordstrom's formative years as a shoe store, few employees were college educated. The second-generation leadership of Everett, Elmer and Lloyd believed it was their duty to create jobs where men (only men at that time) could make a living. In 1952, Nordstrom created a profit-sharing plan to make sure that employees would have money for retirement beyond Social Security, and to help the company attract better personnel. Like everything else at Nordstrom, the profit-sharing plan has built-in financial incentives that encourage industriousness, teamwork, customer service, and expense savings. Loyalty is promoted because employees share ownership. Today, Nordstrom's plan has evolved into a 401K plus a company match.

"It was a natural development that reflected our basic philosophy: the better we treated our people, the better our people performed," wrote Elmer in his book *The Winning Team*.

The Nordstrom system is entrepreneurial. Ever since the early 1950s, when Nordstrom sold only shoes, employee compensation has been based on commissions on net sales. Everett, Elmer and Lloyd knew the best way to attract and retain good people—self-starters who didn't require a lot of supervision— was by paying them according to their ability. Commission sales and bonuses, "gave them added incentive to work harder, and by working harder, they were often able to build a loyal customer following," wrote Elmer.

In the 1960s, after Nordstrom bought Best's Apparel, they became one of the nation's first apparel retailers to pay meaningful sales commission. Eventually, Seattle became the first city in the United States where every major department and specialty store had a system of commission selling.

> In the 1970s, Nordstrom assembled a talented and driven group of women who became role models, inspirations and mentors.

OPPORTUNITIES FOR WOMEN

BECAUSE THE MALE NORDSTROMS OF THE third generation of Bruce, John N., Jim and Jack McMillan recognized they knew little about the women's apparel business, "they were very anxious to identify people who demonstrated a flair for women's apparel and move them along," recalled Cynthia Paur. Launching her Nordstrom career in 1968 doing stock work while still a college student, Paur became the youngest person and the second woman to be named a company vice president.

Nordstrom gradually assembled a talented and driven

group of women who later became role models, inspirations and mentors for all the people in the company.

"This was a pivotal time for women in the workforce in general, and at Nordstrom in particular," said Paur. "There were many jobs available for women. It all depended on what career path you wanted to take, whether it was on the merchant side or the store management side. I always felt that any job I wanted was open to me. The women who were working for the company back then knew that if you wanted to be taken seriously, and if you wanted to have a management position, you were going to have to prove yourself."

In the 1970s, Gail Cottle was part of that group of trailblazing women Nordstrom executives. Gail noted that in those days, "learning how to sell shoes was the precursor for learning how to sell every idea, every plan, everything that required a vote from management. You had to present your merchandise, make your case, make sure it fit the parameters, and then close the sale. They asked enough questions to make you go back and look at your plan again. Once they said they were with you, they let you run your business and play it out. That's a wonderful feeling because you're always going to have a hiccup."

Betsy Sanders joined the company as a salesperson on the selling floor in September 1971, rose up through the organization, and was the first manager of South Coast Plaza mall in Costa Mesa, California, in Orange County, which was Nordstrom's first outpost outside of the Pacific Northwest. She eventually became general manager of the Southern California region. Over a twelve-year period, Sanders and her team built the Southern California business to annual sales of $1 billion ($3.6 billion in today's dollars). After retiring from Nordstrom, Sanders wrote a bestselling book entitled *Fabled*

Service and served as a director on many corporate boards, including Walmart's.

"The Nordstroms recognized the important qualities of women in the organization: gravitas, commitment, connection with the customer," said Sanders. "Many companies choose women for all the wrong reasons. The Nordstroms chose people who didn't see this as just a job. It was all about passion, commitment, and a willingness to break the mold."

Susan Brotman came to Nordstrom in 1973, and ultimately became a member of the Executive Committee. She left the company in 1979 to marry and start a family with her husband Jeffrey Brotman, co-founder of Costco Wholesale.

"After working as a buyer, I was named sales promotion manager, which was an unlikely move, and I was terrified," Susan told me. "But it was very typical of the way Nordstrom operated. They gave people the opportunity to go beyond their training, and beyond what they felt was their capacity. While other companies had formal training programs, Nordstrom just put us all out there to sink or swim. There was a sense of working together as a family toward the same goals."

In this era where parental leave is an expected perk in corporate America, Nordstrom was ahead of the game. Cynthia Paur recalled a time in the 1980s, "when we were all trying to sort out the role of women in the workplace. A couple of women in management were pregnant. I asked Mr. Jim how I should handle that. He said, 'I was talking to the other guys about this over coffee. We don't know. We think it's great that you're in a spot to make that decision because you're a woman. Whatever you think is great with us. It's up to you.'"

THAT is empowerment. THAT is being socially responsible.

Nordstrom has regularly made *Fortune* magazine's lists of the "100 Best Companies to Work For" and "World's Most

Admired Companies; " as well as *Forbes*'s "Top Regarded Companies" and "World's Best Employers" for respectively "New Grads," "Women" and "Diversity" and has been rated a top workplace by the job-matching websites Indeed and Glassdoor.

"The measure of success is your ability to support and enable people to be successful. That's a very satisfying part of the job," said Pete. "If you're going to be successful, it's not because you have all the answers and you're doing all the work. It's surrounding yourself with people that are actually better than you at these things. Once you put your ego aside and let it happen it's super satisfying."

Steve Antle, who had been a career police officer in the Nashville, Tennessee area, sustained an on-the-job injury that eventually led to an addiction to opiate painkillers, sending his life out of control, culminating in a three-year prison term. In 2012, while still in residential probation and not allowed to drive, he applied for a job as a stock clerk at Nordstrom. In March of that year, he was invited by human resources to come in for an interview that lasted over an hour. He was eventually hired, and spent the next years in several jobs, including assistant manager at the Nordstrom Rack in Brentwood, Tennessee.

In 2014, when his store won the company's President's Cup for outstanding performance, Steve was at his desk in the Logistics office when a stranger knocked on the door and introduced himself. "I'm Blake. I've been wanting to meet you." As Steve wrote on the "Friends of Nordstrom" Facebook page in 2019, after Blake's death:

"Turns out . . . Blake had family with addiction issues. My application went all the way to his desk, and he literally 'hired' me. My life changed forever because Nordstrom and Blake took a chance on me, and that job opened so many doors for me. I'm 14 years clean and sober . . . have a lovely wife, my retirement and have had my pick of jobs. I owe Blake a lot and it broke my heart when he died."

> "We can't have a personal connection with customers and employees if we don't have an authentic set of core beliefs and values."

DIVERSITY EQUITY INCLUSION

BEFORE THE RISE OF HOT-BUTTON SOCIAL and political issues in 2020, Nordstrom had always tried to remain neutral and above the fray.

"We grew up being taught to respect all our customers and to the extent that they have different opinions, that means we can't have an opinion on anything that's personal or political," said Pete. "We were always Switzerland [neutral]. We would never offer an opinion. But today, you have to stand up for something. We can't have a personal connection with customers and employees if we don't have an authentic set of core beliefs and values."

A significant number of young people in today's workforce want their place of business to be aligned with their moral and ethical values. Because many employees seek a reason to believe in the company they work for, Nordstrom proactively forges meaningful connections between its millennial associates and the core values of the company; to keep them engaged by offering learning and development opportunities with the emphasis on gaining new experiences.

Nordstrom's Social Responsibility initiatives are centered around diversity in recruiting people at all levels of the company, talent, promoting equity, and creating a more collaborative and communicative culture. To show how seriously Nordstrom views these initiatives, the committee is co-chaired by Erik and Pete.

By 1995, when the first version of *The Nordstrom Way* was published, nearly 30 percent of employees (including 19 percent of management) were people of color. Hispanics or Latinos/Latinas comprised 23 percent of the workforce; Black or African-Americans 19 percent; and Asians/Pacific Islanders 11 percent. Today, women represent 68 percent of all employees; 60 percent of leadership (vice president and above), 36 percent of the executive team, and 45 percent of the board of directors. As of the writing of this book, 60 percent of employees identify as non-white; two of 10 board members are Black.

Alfred Osborne, Professor and Faculty Director at the Price Center for Entrepreneurship & Innovation at UCLA's Anderson School of Management, was selected as Nordstrom's first African-American member of the board of directors back in 1987 and served until 2006. During Blake's ascension to leadership in 2000, Osborne was informally a mentor for Blake.

More than one-third of the models Nordstrom uses in its ads and catalogs are people of color.

In 2019, Nordstrom achieved 100 percent pay equity for employees of all genders and races. Pay equity was evaluated by analyzing base pay to assess whether employees with similar roles, experience and performance earn equal pay for comparable work.

Since 2005, Nordstrom has earned a 100-percent rating on the Human Rights Campaign's annual Corporate Equality Index survey, which rates large U.S. employers on their policies, practices, and benefits related to gay, lesbian, bisexual, and transgender communities and employees, recognizing the company for creating a workplace that is committed to equality for all.

Nordstrom's employees have a choice of eight Employee Resource Groups that, "represent a variety of seen and unseen identities," according to the company, "and offer opportunities to listen and learn."

The company created a Supplier Diversity Program to facilitate business relationships with a more varied pool of vendors of office supplies, food, music, photography and more.

Beginning in the early 1990s, Nordstrom first appeared on the Hispanic 100, a group of companies catering to that community.

Nordstrom's employee sensitivity training program recognizes and affirms the experiences of all employees and customers. Recognizing the needs of physically challenged customers, Nordstrom has improved access in the stores including widening aisles for wheelchairs. Since 1991, Nordstrom has included fashion models with physical disabilities.

In 2020, Aurora James, Creative Director and Founder of luxury accessories brand Brother Vellies, challenged retailers to commit 15 percent of their shelf-space to Black-owned businesses. (Black people make up about 15 percent of the U.S. population.) In August 2022, Nordstrom piloted its first Black Business Month program and created #BuyBlack pop-up markets to highlight a special curation of local Black businesses as well as spotlight the Black-owned or founded brands that it carries year-round. In February 2023, Celebrating Black History Month Nordstrom launched Black/style@Nordstrom, a limited-time pop-up shop at eight Nordstrom locations and online.

In 2023, Nordstrom launched a two-course Product Management track at Morehouse College, a Historically Black College and University based in Atlanta, Georgia. The curriculum, sponsored by Nordstrom, includes a one-credit course on preparing students for technology careers, with direct access to industry professionals; and a three-credit course that focuses on the role of product managers and their potential career paths.

> "We hold ourselves to goals and we call ourselves out when we fall short of our goals."

GIVING BACK TO THE COMMUNITY

NORDSTROM HAS ALWAYS BELIEVED IN the importance of the company and the family to support the communities in which they do business.

"Part of our culture is to do the right thing; not go through a cost/benefit analysis on everything," said Erik. "It's not just the bottom line. There is a synergy to us giving back; to making our communities better. It makes our business better and makes us a better employer. We want to be authentic and transparent. We hold ourselves to goals and we call ourselves out when we fall short of our goals. We should fall short. If you hit every goal, they're not very ambitious goals."

From 2011 to 2013, Nordstrom operated Treasure & Bond, an independent charity-concept store in Manhattan's SoHo neighborhood that donated 100 percent of its profits to New York children's charities and raised more than $200,000. In 2014, Nordstrom launched Treasure & Bond as a private-label brand that donates 2.5 percent of sales to organizations focused on empowering youth.

The company has given away tens of thousands of Nike sneakers distributed to children at elementary schools with a high percentage of students who qualify for free and reduced lunch programs. Nordstrom employees have delivered tens of thousands of new shoes in partnership with Shoes That Fit, a non-profit. When customers purchase a $10.00 giving card during the back-to-school season, they help provide a pair of new, properly fitted athletic shoes to a child at a local elementary school.

For example, in October 2022, Nordstrom volunteer staffers delivered over 275 pairs of new Nike sneakers to students at New York City's Franklin D. Roosevelt Elementary School as a part of their partnership with Shoes That Fit. Nordstrom also brought gift bags for the kids, as well as provided a DJ and a dance party hosted by New York native Kia Vaughn of the Women's National Basketball Association's Atlanta Dream.

At the beginning of the pandemic in early 2020, Nordstrom partnered with Kaas Tailored, a furniture and upholstery manufacturer located north of Seattle, and Seattle's Providence Hospital to create more than 100,000 masks. Nordstrom also collaborated with Missouri-based Ascension Health (a non-profit company that operates a network of hospitals and health facilities) to make nearly one million medical masks. Nordstrom provided the materials to sew into masks that were then returned, sanitized, and distributed throughout the hospital networks. Alterations teams in stores made an additional 60,000 reusable face covers for all employees who were still working to fulfill online orders.

Beginning in the 1950s, the Nordstrom family has worked closely with United Way of King County in their hometown of Seattle. Bruce is a former co-chair of United Way's major gift campaign. Blake and his wife Molly, served as co-chairs of the organization's major gift effort for six years. Each year, many hundreds of Seattle-area Nordstrom employees participate in United Way Day of Caring, completing dozens of service projects throughout King County. In addition, Nordstrom employees annually volunteer tens of thousands of hours of their time.

Nordstrom matches each individual employee's charitable donations, up to $5,000 each year. The company contributes many millions of dollars to hundreds of organizations located in every community where Nordstrom operates.

Blake was also a local leader in the fight against homelessness, supporting for decades the Seattle-based non-profit Plymouth Housing, which provides shelter for adults experiencing rootlessness.

One of Nordstrom's values is "We Extend Ourselves." For decades, Blake kept a laminated card with the words "Extend yourself," which originally came from the Reverend Dale Turner, the late renowned Seattle-based clergyman who was very close to the Bruce Nordstrom family. The company has focused on that value with these words: "We treat each other with respect and kindness. We do the small things that make a big difference. We create a welcoming environment, helping people feel connected, valued and part of one community."

Upon Blake's passing in 2019, the Seattle-based *Puget Sound Business Journal* created the Blake Nordstrom Humanitarian Award for Corporate Giving, which is conferred annually to a Puget Sound area executive who has made a difference. Past winners include Satya Nadella, Chairman and Chief Executive Officer of Microsoft; Phyllis Campbell, chairwoman JPMorgan Chase & Co. Pacific Northwest and a former Nordstrom director; and Laurie Black, CEO of the Boys & Girls Clubs of King County and a former Nordstrom executive.

ENVIRONMENTAL SUSTAINABILITY

MANY EMPLOYEES AND CUSTOMERS FEEL it is important for companies to do good, whether in sustainability or social responsibility. Nordstrom has been communicating more on that front than it ever did in the past.

For example, the company established "Sustainable Style," an online shopping category consisting entirely of items that are sustainably sourced and manufactured in factories that meet the company's social and/or environmental standards. The category comprises more than 2,000 items from 90 brands, including Nordstrom-made Treasure & Bond.

Nordstrom distribution centers recycle on average 98 percent of their waste. Nordstrom has a very vigorous take-back-and-recycle program on packaging of beauty products that are cleaned and separated into metals, glass and plastics, then recycled based on the material composition. The program received the *Good Housekeeping* Sustainable Innovation Award and helped Nordstrom make *Newsweek* magazine's the "Top 500 Greenest Companies in America."

A Different Kind of Community Responsibility

NORDSTROM'S COMMITMENT TO THE COMMUNITY extended to its relationship with the Seattle Seahawks of the National Football League. As mentioned previously, the Nordstrom family was the original majority owner of the team in 1975, then eventually bought out their partners. John N. inherited from his father Elmer the role of representative of the family ownership. The family ran the team until 1988, when they sold it to Kenneth Behring a Northern California businessman. Part of the deal was that Behring promised to never relocate the team out of Seattle.

But on Sunday morning February 2, 1996, moving vans

began hauling equipment out of the Seahawk's headquarters in suburban Kirkland, Washington and headed south on Interstate 5 to Los Angeles, which Behring had unilaterally declared the team's new home. Players were instructed to do their offseason workouts at the Los Angeles Rams' old facility in Anaheim. (This was at a time when the Rams were playing in St. Louis, before eventually moving back to Los Angeles.) Behring's plan was halted when the National Football League threatened to fine him $500,000 a day until he returned the Seahawks to Seattle. An owner can't unilaterally move a team without approval from the other NFL owners. King County (owner of the Kingdome stadium) filed lawsuits against Behring.

John N., who was personally offended by Behring's behavior, sprang into action to find a local owner. He recruited Microsoft co-founder Paul Allen to buy the team in 1997. Under Allen's ownership, John was drafted as a member of the Seahawks Advisory Board and remained an active and vocal supporter of the team.

"The Nordstroms were the best ownership group I've ever been a part of," said Sherman Smith, a former Seahawks running back and coach, in John's book, *Mr. John*. "Mr. Nordstrom gave me the opportunity to learn the business of retail. He was looking out for me. He said, 'Let's talk about what you're going to do after you're done playing football.'"

ON FEBRUARY 2, 2014, THE SEAHAWKS beat the Denver Broncos 43-8 to win the Super Bowl for the first and only time in their history. Two weeks earlier, on January 19, 2014, the Seahawks met their arch-rivals, the San Francisco 49ers, for the National Football Conference Championship at CenturyLink Field in Seattle. The winner would earn the right to go to the Super Bowl.

The Seahawks had asked John N. if he would hand the trophy to Paul Allen if the Seahawks won.

Well, the Seahawks beat the San Francisco 49ers 23-17 in an exciting finish in front of a raucous home crowd. At the conclusion of the game, John was able to make it through the chaos of the celebrating throng and climb onto the stage for the post-game festivities. With the trophy in his hand, John turned to Paul Allen, and said, "On behalf of the National Football League, it is my honor to present you with the George Halas Trophy as the NFC . . . [pause for effect] Champions!!"

And the crowd of 68,454 roared their approval.

Now THAT'S customer service.

And those are the F.A.C.T.S.

TAKEAWAYS

- Be public about your core beliefs and values

- Make your company a desirable place to work

- Support and enable your people to be successful

- Offer learning and developmental opportunities and new experiences

- Give back to the community/communities in which you do business

- Be environmentally aware

- Help protect human rights

- Extend yourself

Acknowledgments

First and foremost, a heartfelt collective thank-you to Nordstrom—both the family and the company. Over the past four-plus decades, I've had the opportunity to interview members of three of the four generations of the family leadership: Elmer, Bruce, John, Jim N., Blake, Pete, Erik, and Jamie Nordstrom and Jack McMillan.

Thanks to their trust and generosity, I have been given unique access to many company executives, directors and, most important, frontline people who all shared the company's inner workings, philosophies, thoughts and strategies.

In particular, I am eternally grateful to chairman emeritus Bruce Nordstrom who honored me by asking for my assistance with the writing of his memoir, *Leave It Better Than You Found It*, published in 2007 and revised in 2022. Over the decades, Bruce and I spent countless hours talking about the two things closest to his heart: family and company. I look back on those sessions with great fondness.

I am also grateful to the company for allowing me to use the picture of founder John W. on the cover of this book.

Thanks to Scott Meden, Geevy Thomas, Michael Koppel, Bob Schwartz, Alfred Osborne, and Jesse James Barnholt for their insight on Nordstrom, past and present.

Thanks to Nina Diamond for her early reading of the manuscript and her insightful comments.

Thanks to Melissa Coffman and Scott Book of Book House Publishing for putting this book together.

Thanks to Keith Bendis, my friend for more a half a century, who created the illustrations for this book.

All my love and affection to my darling companion, Gerri Dale.

And thanks to all the Nordies who have helped to create a company with a reputation for customer service that is envied throughout the world.

Robert Spector
Bellingham, WA

About the Author

ROBERT SPECTOR IS THE AUTHOR OF a series of books under the umbrella title of *The Nordstrom Way*. He assisted chairman emeritus Bruce Nordstrom with his memoir, *Leave It Better Than You Found It*, originally published in 2007 and revised and updated in 2022.

He is also the author of *Amazon.com: Get Big Fast*, the first book on the company, published in 2000, and *The Mom & Pop Store: True Stories From the Heart of America*, which is part road story and part memoir of working as a teenager is his father's butcher shop in Perth Amboy, New Jersey. He has also written many published corporate histories of notable companies such as Pizza Hut, Kimberly Clark and Eddie Bauer.

Robert has taught a retail elective at the University of Washington and Western Washington University. He is a graduate of Perth Amboy High School (where he is a member of the Hall of Fame) and Franklin & Marshall College.

A sought-after keynote speaker, Robert has educated audiences on Nordstrom in 28 countries. He lives in Bellingham, WA.

To learn more and/or to book Robert as a speaker, please visit www.TheRobertSpector.com.

Robert can be reached at Robert@TheRobertSpector.com.